Developments in

Early Childhood Education

Janet Lancaster and Joan Gaunt

Open Books
London

First published in 1976 by Open Books Publishing Ltd,
87–89 Shaftesbury Avenue, LONDON W1V 7AD

© Janet Lancaster and Joan Gaunt 1976

Hardback: ISBN 0 7291 0027 8

Paperback: ISBN 0 7291 0022 7

Text set in 11/12 pt Photon Imprint, printed by photolithography, and
bound in Great Britain at The Pitman Press, Bath

26. OCT. 1994

10. NOV. 1994

Developments in Early Childhood Education

The Changing Classroom

General Editor: John Eggleston

Contents

Editor's introduction

The theme of this series of books is the changing classroom. Everyone knows that schools change – that despite all the influences of tradition things aren't the same as they used to be. Yet during the past decade the change has been on such an unprecedented scale that in many ways schools have become surprising places not only to those who work with them – like parents and employers – but even to those who work in them, like teachers and students.

There are many reasons for these changes. Some are organisational, like the move to comprehensive secondary schooling, the raising of the school leaving age, new pre-school classes, and 'de-streaming', where children of all abilities work together. But even more spring from the way the teachers works in the classroom – from the increasing emphasis on individual methods, on creativity rather than remembering, on new patterns of assessment and examination, and on the use of a wide variety of project methods.

Such changes have certainly transformed the life of many classrooms and made school a different place for teachers and their students. This series is about life in those classrooms, for it is here that we can not only see change but understand it and get to grips with its effects on young people and on the society in which they will live.

In this volume Janet Lancaster and Joan Gaunt review new developments in early childhood education. They show that in this formative period of development a great revolution has occurred – a revolution that has had a profound impact upon almost all areas of schooling. They show how teachers have become increasingly sensitive to the needs of young children; how learning has become genuinely child centred so that individualised learning has replaced class instruction; how relationships in the classroom became based on partnerships rather than on control. But how do the new approaches work out in practice? Are they appropriate for all teachers and all children? Are children adequately motivated in a relaxed system? Are basic skills in reading, writing and number work effectively achieved? Janet Lancaster and Joan Gaunt, both experienced teachers of young children, answer these questions with a highly informative account of the new early childhood education.

John Eggleston

Introduction

In this book we have tried to show trends in educational practice which reflect some of the current thinking about young children's development and learning. The focus has been upon practice within schools, both that which precedes the statutory school age of five, and that which follows within the infant or first school, thus including the years from three to eight. Provision for the pre-school child is variable and in any case cannot be viewed as desirable on a compulsory basis for every child. Such provision would be seen to be complementary to the home and not as a substitute for it. Although the emphasis is upon children in the classroom the latter can no longer be considered as a tightly enclosed place uninfluenced by outside happenings or by a child's experience beyond the school walls. Thus the major move towards deeper understanding of the relationship of home, school and community and the desirability of forging strong links between them is stressed.

We would like to thank all the teachers and children who have indirectly contributed to this book and especially the teacher who shared with us her class building site study. The names of children have been changed but all references to them and to classroom experiences are based on real situations.

PART I

1 Nursery and infant education: an historical perspective

Early influences upon the development of early childhood education

So many things seem to have started with the Greeks! No less a person than Plato considered that children should be removed from their homes at an early age and be looked after by people specially trained in the care and education of young children. So much for the idea that mothers know instinctively what is right for their children. Comenius, a bishop of the Moravian Church, took an opposing view and designed a programme for mothers to use in the home, although he too stressed the importance of early influences and impressions. Rousseau in the mid eighteenth century forwarded the then novel idea that children were not miniature adults imbued with original sin but natural beings in their own right who needed unburdened freedom to grow and develop. His book *Emile* was seized upon by the *avant garde* of the nineteenth century and some middle and upper class children had an *Emile*-type upbringing in their earliest years. However, the basic philosophy of freedom of expression was considered neither appropriate nor applicable for the masses and scarcely affected their prevailing 3R curriculum, best described as regimentation, rigour and rote, superimposed with harsh discipline.

Continental influences on the British educational system were of the utmost importance. However, their passage into what has come to be accepted as 'good practice' in early childhood education has been erratic and spasmodic. Perhaps one of the greatest debts is to Froebel. As long ago as 1826 he was emphasising that play was the basis of early learning. Froebel had worked under the guidance of Pestalozzi and later was the first person to formulate a comprehensive concept of pre-school education. He considered that early education was always related to and supplementary to the educational influence of the home. Pestalozzi had in his turn been strongly influenced by Rousseau and applied many of his theories in the running of his school. However, he considered some of Rousseau's ideas gave a child the insecurity of too much freedom and so he emphasised the need for teacher guidance. Shades of this confusion between freedom for children and the teacher's guidance of children's discoveries still prevail. Both Pestalozzi and Froebel firmly believed in basing any form of instruction upon the children's own concrete experiences.

Robert Owen

Pestalozzi's school in Switzerland attracted many visitors. Among them was a remarkable Welshman, Robert Owen. He managed the New Lanark cotton mills and opened the first British nursery infant school there in 1816 as part of the services and provision for the mill workers. He was visionary yet practical, abhorring the impoverishment and exploitation of the working classes. He saw that the major route to alleviate these problems was through education, which in turn would influence social reform. The school was innovatory in many ways. It took children from the age of two until they left at ten to work in the mill. The organisation, disciplinary methods and curriculum were clearly child-centred. The following passage indicates the level of considerate and thoughtful planning. In it Owen explains the instructions he gave to the two untrained teachers, James Buchanan and Molly Young:

They were on no account ever to beat any one of the children, or to threaten them in any manner of word or action, or to use abusive terms; but were always to speak to them with a pleasant countenance, and in a kind manner and tone of voice. That they should tell the infants and children that they must on all occasions do all they could to make their playfellows happy.... The school room ... was furnished with paintings, chiefly of animals, with maps, and often supplied with natural objects from the gardens, fields and woods – the examination of which always excited their curiosity and created an animated conversation between the children and their instructors. (Owen 1857)

To discourage the early formalisation of instruction, books were excluded from the classrooms for the two- to six-year-olds. Books were in any case few and far between in those days. Each day the children spent three hours in the playground. Singing, dancing, marching, playing ring games and fife-playing were included in the curriculum. The inclusion of dancing perhaps indicates an early example of insight into children's home environments and the need to foster links between the community and school.

If only Owen's influence had developed fully, radical advances would have been made, particularly in the education of the under-fives. As it happened these had to wait until the twentieth century for it was Wilderspin who promoted the establishment of infant schools and became the major influence upon early childhood education in nineteenth-century England. He taught at Spitalfields Infant School and became the agent of the London Infant School Society, formed in 1824 to develop schools and teacher training. He lacked Owen's insight and had little understanding of developmental approaches. Wilderspin stressed reliance upon book information, rote learning and general 'chalk and talk' methods. The untrained teachers of young children of the day were under pressure because of 'payment by results' – a method of inspection where children's factual knowledge was tested on rote-learned answers. This tended to make their pupils submissive and thus prepared them for the formalised instruction of the monitorial schools. Here we see the reinforcement of one of the four main elements that make up attitudes towards the role of education in the early years, namely the insistence upon rigorously formal instruction. The other three are the physical and social welfare element, didactic behaviourist approaches and child-centred methods.

1 Formal instructional methods

This method of imparting knowledge by instruction through rote and mass 'learning', which regards children not as individuals but as so many empty vessels to be filled with facts, still has credibility with many teachers. What needs to be remembered is that this method developed in the nineteenth century when there were huge classes, no trained teachers as such, payment by results (which clearly narrowed the curriculum) and very little understanding of children's needs. It meant that large groups of children could be controlled and instructed with ease. For most children such approaches were, and still are, totally unsuitable, for there is nothing in them to which the child can respond – it is like trying to stick facts on to non-adhesive children. (This is not to suggest that formal methods should never be used, but that they should form one facet of a multiplicity of approaches.) The advocates of this method feel it ensures good standards, and parents, the majority of whom are most familiar with this approach, may not appreciate how high teacher domination must be to make it effective. This high degree of direction can mean that most early work is merely a facsimile of that of the teacher. The child's originality and intense desire to explore can thus readily be stifled. It is perhaps easy to see why many teachers of young children have consistently fought against anything that smacks of formalised instruction, for stories proliferate of the early days of state education where children as young as three and four were cramped at tiered desks for hours, perhaps chanting one letter of the alphabet 120 times on end.

2 The physical and social welfare element

The second element concerns those educationists who focused upon the improvement of the physical and social welfare aspects of children's lives. Much of their effort was concentrated in the nursery school, a school for children below the statutory school age of five. This approach arose because of the urgent necessity to alleviate the desperate social conditions of many children. It gained tremendous momentum and credence in the first three decades of this century, largely due to the work of two sisters, Rachel and Margaret McMillan. They recognised that under-nourished, tired, probably verminous, dirty children were in no sense in a receptive state for 'education'. They pioneered the remarkable advances which have taken place in medical inspection, in hygienic facilities such as school showers and better ventilation in classrooms. Although they were unsuccessful in obtaining free school meals Margaret was largely responsible for the Act starting school meals. This strict routine of physical care and welfare meant school days punctuated by fresh air, sleep, baths and food. It was an essential and imperative approach in those days of deplorable social conditions. Unfortunately this strict adherence to regimes of cleanliness routines became entrenched in some nursery teachers' attitudes, sometimes at the expense of consideration of children's intellectual development. This is not to suggest that the McMillans themselves neglected the development of the intellect, for they were anxious to extend their influence beyond the level of physical care. However, Margaret McMillan shared the prevailing fears that one method of stultifying and cramping children's 'imaginations', the formal element, was about to be replaced by another more rationally considered one.

3 The didactic behaviourist element

The influence that Margaret McMillan deplored resulted from Maria Montessori's work. A doctor and psychologist, Montessori based her methods upon those used by Séguin, whose work had been with mentally handicapped children. Montessori devised simple apparatus for sensory training and for teaching mathematical concepts. This involved stimulus-response training and a rigorous sequence of learning events which left little scope for individuality, even though each child had his own apparatus. It was over-structured and heavily teacher-directed and did not leave the teacher free to adapt her approaches. The method, if strictly adhered to, used the teacher as a robot. Moreover it is frequently said that the apparatus did not present children with enough challenges. Montessori's methods had the strongest influence in the private sector but her genius for devising techniques does have relevant implications for aspects of today's curriculum in state schools where some children may need a precisely structured element in their early education.

Although these comments have greatly simplified their underlying ideas, these approaches still influence current practice. Each of them, in varying degrees, has hindered and helped the development of a number of approaches to individuals and the curriculum. It was not until Susan Isaacs's work that a fourth element emerged. This upgraded the concept of education and formed a basis and direction for new developments.

4 Child-centred approaches

Susan Isaacs was a psychologist who strongly emphasised the importance of the development of the intellect in young children. The study of man and his behaviour was gaining enormous impetus in the 1920s. Susan Isaacs studied the work of the psychoanalysts and based many of her interpretations of children's behaviour on Freud's work. Fortunately for the development of early childhood education in this country she rejected the narrow behaviourist approaches prevalent at the time. As Whitbread states, 'her rejection of the narrow behaviourist psychology that was then fashionable, and her emphasis on language and reasoning were of fundamental importance for the evolution of a sound pedagogical approach to nursery education' (Whitbread 1972). She also helped to establish the concept of early childhood education outside the realms of sentiment and evangelism (although the latter is sometimes difficult to avoid when provision of state nursery education never seems to meet the demand). She studied individual differences in intellectual, social and emotional growth, and produced a defined pedagogy. The list of equipment for the Malting House School, started in 1924, which Susan Isaacs ran, remains an interesting model for equipping a present-day nursery school.

The provisions for early childhood education

Regrettably, alongside this pioneering work a rapid decline took place in the numbers of two- to four-year-olds receiving state education. Surprisingly, in the late nineteenth and early twentieth century large numbers of young children attended school. In 1900 43 per cent of three- to five-year-olds received some education. Why was this so? It resulted not from any great educational conviction but largely because working mothers had no one to look after their younger children if their older children attended school. Some teachers resigned themselves to it, realising that if they refused to take these younger children the older ones would not attend at all. Others viewed it as compensation for parents losing the earnings of their older children, who were compelled to attend school. However, one result of all these young children being in school was that they, the 'babies', were placed in separate classrooms. It was even suggested that their education became so much more like amusement that they were inadequately prepared for the next, more rigorous phase of their schooling. Versions of this criticism are still to be found, as are references to the youngest reception classes as the 'babies' class. Tradition, as they say, dies hard!

In 1905 women Inspectors of the Board of Education, dismayed by the type of education generally offered to the under-fives, recommended the provision of nursery schools where a more appropriate education might be obtained. By 1907 it became the Board of Education's policy to encourage the exclusion of the under-fives from school. This was not counter-balanced by the provision of nursery schools. Although this policy ousted much early childhood education from the public sector it did provide an opportunity for experimentation and the development in private schools of flexible attitudes and approaches which were so frequently impeded in other sectors of education.

The Hadow Report 1933

This report (Board of Education 1933) by the consultative committee on infant and nursery schools provided a compelling rationale for the extension of nursery school provision. It noted the influence of Froebel, Montessori and the McMillans and emphasised that in the best nursery schools methods were eclectic, combining features from various sources. The report's comments upon the hoped-for extension of nursery school influence up through the system indicate a reinforcement of the separatism of pre-school education. It clearly feared that any re-amalgamation at that time might erode the generally more appropriate approaches to the 'whole child' prevalent in the nursery school:

We hope that the valuable ideas embodied in the nursery school will increasingly be realised within the existing infant school system. Meanwhile it seems highly desirable that the nursery school should be developed separately, and be left free to perfect its methods, and to fulfil its special purpose. The infant school has, admittedly, suffered in the past from bookish and academic traditions. The nursery school is one means of counteracting these influences, by extending upwards its own special tradition of health, reasonable freedom, and joyful spontaneous pursuits. (Board of Education 1933, para. 77)

Do those who wish to see the nursery school continue as a separate institution still share some of these fears?

2 The growth of the first school

Present-day provision for the under-fives

Today education of children below statutory school age takes place in various types of institution in both the maintained and independent sectors. The Department of Education and Science statistics in January 1974 were as follows:

Number of children aged two to four years attending school or other educational institutions in England and Wales:

Maintained	Full-time	Part-time
Nursery schools	15,209	30,401
Nursery classes	32,527	61,762
Pre-rising-fives in reception classes	268,531	16,089
Total maintained	424,519	
Independent		
Playgroups	250,000 (estimated)	
Nursery schools	1,192	1,950
Total independent	253,142	
TOTAL	677,661	

It is interesting to note that over 66 per cent of the places in the maintained sector were for the group referred to as 'pre-rising-five-year-olds' (children just over four years old) in reception classes in infant, first or primary schools. This area of provision poses many problems. Usually the children have only one teacher and their equipment, spatial and other facilities may be inadequate in comparison with many nursery schools and classes. The biggest contrast is between the two adult : child ratios; many infant teachers regret that they have to cope with thirty to forty four-year-olds with minimal ancillary support, when the nursery teacher has two qualified nursery nurses, often students in training, as well as a cook and caretaker more closely involved in interaction with the children (in fact a ratio of at least one adult per thirteen children). The fact that government cuts in education (September 1975) included the proposal that Local Authorities save money by stopping under- and pre-rising-fives attending primary schools exacerbates the situation, for it lessens the supply of places when public demand is higher than ever. It can also be argued that even with these limited facilities, the skilled infant teacher can do much to enrich the experiences of young children and help to alleviate some of the pressure on mothers.

A major problem associated with incorporating the education of the under-fives in existing primary schools is that the community and occasionally the teachers associate the building with all the formal expectations of 'school'. Subsequently there can be pressure upon teachers to teach formal skills before some children are sufficiently mature. This is the 'downward' influence that led the 1933 Hadow committee to plead for the maintenance of separate institutions.

The playgroup movement

The dearth in maintained provision has led to the rapid expansion of independent playgroups. The playgroup movement is financed by parental contributions, grants from voluntary organisations and various kinds of support from local education authorities. Many teachers viewed this provision as a stop-gap until maintained provision became adequate. The movement is well-established, has its staunch supporters and will therefore need to be integrated with any future developments. The pre-school playgroup movement is an excellent example of the success of mutual self-help within communities, for the movement is manned, funded and supported almost entirely by parents. Originally the majority of groups were run by middle class parents for their own children but now more than half of them have a qualified supervisor. The groups function for a few hours in the mornings or afternoons, which excludes the involvement of full-time working mothers. However, registered child minders, and unregistered ones too, for that matter, who may be looking after the children of such mothers, are encouraged to take their groups along for some sessions. The quality of the provision varies tremendously, and there can be complex problems if the groups are run by mothers who have no professional training. A well-organised playgroup can do much to help the child's integration into the primary school. Conversely, where the lack of official status and professionalism of the mothers impedes their interaction with their neighbours' children, harm can be done which makes the professional teacher's job more not less difficult. Unless the worth of good social play provision is fully appreciated there may be pressure for these very young children to be taught reading skills, perhaps to compete with some local 'cramming' private kindergarten. However, it is important to stress that many of the group leaders now have the opportunity to attend specifically designed local education authority courses. Although the groups are predominantly run for middle class children, voluntary organisations like the Save the Children Fund employ professional staff who run nursery play groups in several areas of special social need.

Pressure for places in maintained nursery schools

The level of present-day provision means that many maintained nursery places are given to children with special needs. This results not only in great pressure and competition for places but frequently means that a nursery group is disproportionately full of children with one form of social handicap or another. This distortion creates several problems and clearly has an effect on the results of any evaluation of the achievements of nursery-educated children.

Present-day provision for the five- to eight-year-olds

The statutory age for starting school is five, although as the statistics show many children start school before that. A child can begin his compulsory schooling in an infant, first or primary school. An infant school takes children until they are seven, when they are transferred to the junior school. Some children attend first schools where they stay until they are eight, nine or in a few cases ten before they move to a middle school. Other children, frequently in more rural areas, attend primary schools where children from five to eleven are catered for. Indeed there has been a reduction in the proportion of children who are educated in separate infant schools largely as a more deliberate policy of viewing education in units covering wider age ranges. In 1925 the proportion of five-year-olds in infant schools was 70 per cent, by 1965 it had dropped to 56 per cent (Central Advisory Council for Education (England) 1967, para. 261). There are clear implications here about the direction initial and in-service training should take, and about the need for primary head-teachers to have considerable knowledge of the social and educational needs of the youngest children.

Certain geographical and traditional factors influence the age of entry. Many areas of Wales for example have a tradition of accepting the pre-rising-fives into school. The system, however, is uneven and unfair, for many children in other parts of the country are not accepted until the term which follows their fifth birthday. Summer-born children, by mere accident of birthdate, will only receive six terms' education in the infant school – for children are transferred to the junior school if they are seven years old on or before the first of September. This is in sharp contrast with others who have well over three years in these schools. The Plowden Committee noted these discrepancies and firmly recommended that the infant school period should be a full three years, with children starting school at the beginning of the school year after they are five. This would mean first schools for five- to eight-year-olds. The recommendation was made for a variety of reasons, a major one being that this length would extend the strong developmental influence of the approaches in many infant schools. If implemented, it would also counteract the problem of summer-born children who, because of their shorter time in the infant school, have sometimes been thought of as 'slow' learners in the junior school. The responses of teachers and children to this form of labelling result in an escalation of the problem.

The Report also recommended a flexible approach to the length of the school day, suggesting that half a school day up to the age of six would be best for some children, although this latter adaptation would require legislation. The implementation of these working recommendations will not be possible until nursery education is available for all who want it.

The strong support given for child-centred education implies a corresponding growth in all types of ancillary help. Nursery nurses, who work in nursery schools, nursery classes, primary schools and playgroups take a two-year training, usually when they are sixteen. Their course consists of theoretical work based on children's developmental needs for two-fifths of their time and practical experience for three-fifths. At the end of two years students sit the examination of the National Nursery Examination Board (N.N.E.B.). The fact that the National Nursery Examination Board syllabus was extended ten years ago for work with children up to seven years should also be an advantage, although clearly large numbers of people will still have to be trained to cope with the staffing requirements in the expanded nursery programme and in the early stages of primary schooling.

The Plowden Report, despite some criticisms, was welcomed by the progressives and innovators as highly supportive evidence of the effectiveness, appropriateness and relevance of their methods and organisation. The report stressed the need for flexibility in provisions and transfer ages, according to the individual child's progress, and gave its sanction to far-reaching amendments to practices then prevailing. Its recommendations for the expansion of nursery education and the direction it should take are in paragraph 343 of the report. It suggested that:

(a) Provision should be made for children to attend morning or afternoon sessions, and 15 per cent of the places for the country as a whole should be for full-time attendance; this meant that the full-time places could be concentrated in areas where there was a particular need. (Our increasing knowledge concerning biological rhythms might indicate that children attending for afternoon sessions only may well receive less adequate stimulation and attention.)

(b) Admissions to the infant school should be staggered over half a term to facilitate happy integration into school (in practice there are head teachers who know the 'words but not the tune', and indeed have a staggered intake which is staggered by mere ten-minute intervals over the first school day); introduction to nursery education should also be gradual.

(c) Local authorities should be given power to assist voluntary nursery groups which should be subject to inspection by local authority and H. M. Inspectorate.

(d) Services relating to the care and education of young children should be grouped near homes and primary schools and such needs should be catered for in new and re-development areas. (Following the latter recommendations community schools, where clinics, libraries, children's centres and other facilities are grouped together, have been built.)

The report proposed that part-time attendance should remain possible after the child reached statutory school age and that a 'nursery type of education would have to be available in the infant schools for those children who still need it'. Just as important, perhaps more so, was the need, when preparing the curriculum, for 'sufficient stimulus in the nursery group for the older and more advanced children'. The term 'older', when we are consistently pleading for suitable levels of curriculum provision for individuals, is not the contradiction it appears to be initially, for sometimes in nursery and primary schools it is hard to distinguish any progression and difference in curriculum content between the first and second year.

An important emphasis was placed upon the need for, and desirability of, close parental involvement and liaison between home and school. This will be discussed in chapter 4.

The 1972 White Paper

This paper, *Education: A Framework for Expansion*, provided for dramatic expansion of pre-school provision. It followed the guidelines recommended by the Plowden and Gittins Reports in 1967. Details of the desired form the expansion should take were subsequently published in Circular 2/73 'Nursery Education' (Department of Education and Science 1973). The government aimed at providing places for 75 per cent of four-year-olds and 35 per cent of three-year-olds by 1982. Nursery education would be made available for all children whose parents wanted it from the beginning of the term after their third birthday until a term after their fifth birthday. It was emphasised that moving four-year-olds up into reception classes was undesirable both on the grounds that it eroded the child's length of stay in the nursery school and because of the problems associated with the narrow age-range of three- and four-year-olds left behind. Although part-time attendance was considered to be most suitable, some flexibility would be necessary to meet the needs of rural children. The suggestion was that perhaps they could attend a nursery on a full-time basis three days a week.

The concept of the first school

The historical perspective, the theories of several pioneers in early childhood education, the Plowden Report and increasing understanding of child development brought about by past and recent research leads us to reassess the nature and content of early childhood education.

Support for extending the age range of early education has come from various sources. Fifty years ago the Independent Labour Party advocated 'the setting up of Nursery Schools for all children from two to seven years of age and the progressive disappearance, as they were set up, of Infant departments'. The McMillans considered that schools from two to eight or nine years were desirable on developmental grounds and Montessori spoke of the need for sequential continuity for three- to seven-year-old children. (Clearly our knowledge of attachment behaviour would make us dispute the separation of two-year-olds from their mothers unless there were exceptional circumstances.) Various events have helped to relax the pressure for academic achievement in this age range, including the final abolition of the Elementary Code by the 1944 Education Act and the abolition of the 11+ exam in areas where a fully comprehensive secondary education system has been introduced. This has meant that infant teachers, especially, have taken advantage of the opportunity to experiment and adopt many of the good nursery school practices. The strong arguments projected by the Plowden and Gittins Reports (Central Advisory Council for Education (England) 1967; Central Advisory Council for Education (Wales) 1967) in support of a full three years in the infant school, with subsequent later transfer to the next stage, mean that teachers and children are given extra time to work without pressure for achievement in a narrow skill sense.

One comparatively recent development has been the establishment of 'first schools'. These schools, which cater for five- to eight- or nine-year-olds (a few cater for tens as well which seems to push the concept too far), mean that children are less likely to be changing schools when they are immature and lacking in competence and confidence. Above all an extended age range provides greater opportunity for teachers to allow for individual maturational rates and variations in social and family background. Some of these first schools incorporate nursery classes or have nursery schools on site, thus extending the age range down to three. Because of the need for a greater consistency of approach, nursery and infant stages will tend to be dovetailed along these lines in a programme of expansion. It would be desirable if the schools could be adjacent to help foster close liaison, or ideally be first schools for three- to eight-year-olds.

Traditionally the nursery school curriculum has been informal (for the constraints and downward pressure from junior, secondary schools and 11+ examinations felt in the infant schools never really applied to the pre-school non-statutory sector). The teaching has revolved around the children's self-chosen activities and play situations. The methods have either been purposeful or incidental (where they are propelled by the child's own innate curiosity without any form of teacher intervention beyond that at the caretaker level). This is in contrast with the concept of 'school' where the emphasis is upon 'verbal instruction, the mastery of symbol systems and systematic instruction in bodies of knowledge' (Tizard 1975). The usefulness of the first school is that it can minimise the sharpness of the differences between these two concepts. Parents and communities tend to perpetuate and emphasise these distinctions largely because efforts to inform parents of developments in the educational content and processes of school are by no means standard practice. Would a fusing of the two types of provision help general understanding of the child and the educational process? And might an extension of the strong parent-teacher liaison of the nursery school facilitate and extend this understanding into the higher age ranges? Clearly a first school could continue to encourage self-directed activities and the freedom to organise one's own experience, but at the same time 'play', to the teacher, should have more specific connotations and objectives. The emphasis should be on developing experiences and through them the skills. Many infant schools already have these approaches well-established but it must be remembered that the Plowden Committee considered that only a third of our children attended schools defined as 'quite clearly good'. There may have been some spread of ideas since, but this still leaves approximately two thirds of children attending schools of lower quality – from schools markedly out of touch with current practice to those with weaknesses yet which are distinguished by specially good personal relationships (Plowden Report, para. 267–276). Although subjective, this type of survey reveals trends and puts the availability of innovatory educational provision for children in a proper perspective.

3 Development and learning in the first school years

It is perhaps only when we look at the present state of the education of young children in this country and compare it with that at the turn of the century that we are able to see the extent of the changes that have gradually taken place. The ideals of educational thinkers, though sometimes very slow to be translated into practice, have nevertheless been reflected in methods, approaches, curriculum content and organisation. Infant and nursery schools have shown themselves ready to experiment, and to take into account new research findings and current thinking in their planning. There has been a great advance in recent years in our understanding of the ways in which children develop and learn, and the good school bases its work firmly upon this knowledge of children and their educational needs.

Among the major developments of the past fifty years has been an increasing emphasis upon the all-round needs of the individual child, as opposed to the 'standard' of the class as a whole, and the introduction of much more freedom of choice of activities (Gardner and Cass, 1965). The importance of play in learning has been recognised to a far greater degree, the distinction between play and work for young children is less clearly defined, and children's own purposes and interests are seen as centrally relevant to their learning. The Plowden Report (paragraphs 278–89) gives illuminating composite pictures of three schools 'run successfully on modern lines' which highlight the purposeful child-centred climate in which children can learn about living with others and extend their understanding of themselves and the world around them in addition to acquiring the foundations of the skills which our society demands.

The uniqueness of the individual

Underlying the move away from the class as the main, if not the only, unit of teaching has been the increasing awareness of the child as a person in his own right, with his own strengths and weaknesses, interests, potential and problems. He becomes the person he is through a continuous network of interactions between two strong and extremely complex forces – heredity and environment. By the time a young child enters the nursery or infant school he will have encountered a range of experiences which he will have absorbed in ways unique to him, because of his own particular make-up. It is well known that even very young babies show markedly different reactions to stimuli, and researches have indicated that some modes of response tend to persist into later life, contributing to characteristic ways of dealing with people or circumstances. Some children, for example, exhibit greater tolerance than others in the face of frustration, some accept defeat more passively while others will show remarkable persistence in mastering a problem. The environments in which children grow up exhibit in their turn a wide diversity, and, in spite of educational and social welfare services, it would be unrealistic to assume that every child reaches school with that 'rich background of experience' of which we often talk.

Observations of individual children over an extended period of time have added to our knowledge of their different rates of development. Each child is likely to experience periods of rapid progress or little apparent advance in some directions, and there will be in any group a number who in one or more aspects are advanced or retarded in relation to the average for their chronological age. Indeed, the latter is often a poor indicator of the kind of situation which will most benefit a child in school. There will be some who learn more slowly, others who grow and mature physically less rapidly and still others who need more time and experience in order to come to terms with their own emotions or with playing and working with other children. The teacher of young children needs to be aware of this unevenness of advance in order to be able to give support and help where it is most needed. Her time is planned to allow for individual or small group teaching. She makes sure, for example, that a child whose language development is poor has plenty of direct experiences about which he will want to talk, and she is careful to create opportunities for him to talk with her as well as with other children. She recognises the value of practice and consolidation, and ideally will provide a wide range of suitable books and materials so that each child may proceed at his own rate and according to his own style of learning. The teacher's organisation allows for drawing together groups as a specific teaching point arises, and these groups may remain stable for as long as their purpose is valid. When they are no longer useful, as some children will have progressed beyond them and others will require more practice, they will be disbanded. Different groupings may apply in different areas of the curriculum to take into account the variation in aptitudes and interests which affect achievement.

Sequence of development

In general, although there are such dramatic differences among children, development proceeds in a similar pattern for all. It is a continuous process in which success at any level depends upon how well the previous levels have been mastered. The adage 'It's no use trying to run before you can walk' is founded upon a sound developmental principle! This similarity of sequence enables us to make certain predictions concerning children's needs at various stages, and provision in school can be based broadly upon this knowledge. The teacher who is aware of 'norms' of development has also a useful yardstick against which she can judge whether special help should be given, and she can then adapt her teaching accordingly. The kinds of equipment, content of books and stories and the type of method or approach used depend upon her understanding of the response it is reasonable to expect from the majority of children of a particular group. She will know, for example, that it is not unusual for the youngest children in a nursery school to play alone. They are often very much concerned with themselves and their own pursuits. After all they have not yet known themselves as persons with separate identities for very long, and still view the world largely from their own standpoint. The teacher will ensure that opportunities arise which encourage contact and interaction with other children. Co-operation and general give-and-take come gradually, but by the time a child leaves the first school at eight or nine years of age he is turning much more towards his contemporaries. Thus group activities are more profitable and enjoyable at this stage, and this is shown in the children's ability to work on common topics within which there is still scope for individual interest and contribution.

Some of the youngest children will find it difficult to share not only materials and toys but the attention of the adult. They are still very dependent upon the reassuring support of parents, and of teachers and other adults in the school situation. This is provided for within the nursery school by a more generous staffing allowance which facilitates the forming of more intimate 'family' units. Frequently the youngest children in the infant school have the greater share of the time of the teacher's aide, and the flexibility of programme, grouping and organisation allows for extra contact with the teacher where it is most needed, on a one-to-one basis. Most healthy children are eager to move towards greater independence, however, and the school will be able to encourage this in relatively safe circumstances. The eight-year-old is likely to be able to establish good relationships with both adults and his own age group, and is beginning to depend increasingly on the latter for approval. This, too, will be taken into account when group activities are being planned.

The concept of the 'whole child'

The concept of the 'whole child' is based upon an understanding that all aspects of human development are interrelated, and that considering single areas in isolation would be absurd, except for its convenience for purposes of study. Change and development in any aspect is likely to have some effect on other areas. For example, the effect of early or late physical maturity has repercussions in the expectations of parents, teachers and contemporaries. The tall boy of good physique may be expected to behave in a more mature fashion than he is in fact capable of, the little girl who looks immature may be treated almost as a doll by other girls in her group. Too great a pressure may be placed upon a child who is intellectually able, and this may prove too much for his present emotional stage of development. If he becomes worried and over-anxious, his ability to learn must be adversely affected, for over-anxiety is a very poor motivator. The child who is unable to cope with his emotions may find difficulty in establishing relationships and may therefore be deprived of the very interchanges which would contribute to his learning. If the aim of helping each child towards achieving his full potential is to be realised these close associations must be considered. This implies an intimate knowledge of each child's progress and of the factors which contribute to it. In practical terms, opportunity for individual informal contacts between teacher and child, exchange of information among teachers and keeping good records of all aspects of development are essential.

The curriculum

Crucial to the all-round development of the child is the provision of a wide variety of experiences. The school tries to provide first of all the best possible conditions for physical growth, bearing in mind the basic need for fresh air, a balanced diet and exercise. Through physical play, and for the older children through more planned physical education periods, the child is given plenty of opportunity to move about and to practise his growing range of skills. As his coordination develops, greater precision and speed of movement are achieved, which help him become confident in his abilities. Care is taken that periods of vigorous activity are followed by quieter occupations.

The growth of children's emotional life is helped by those areas of the curriculum which give insights into the feelings of others, such as story-telling. Most valuable of all, however, are the social contacts which take place in the informal school setting. It is partly for this reason that children are encouraged to move about freely and to talk to each other at most times of the day. They learn to live together, as they learn so many things, by gaining experience in doing so.

The important role of language has been emphasised in the research of sociologists and psychologists over the past decade. Currently, researchers are exploring more effective techniques of helping all children use language more flexibly, with the needs of those whose pre-school background has been meagre being especially considered. The climate of the first school, in which experiences are shared and relationships with contemporaries and adults are formed is conducive to building language skills, and the curriculum is planned to further this objective.

Opportunity for intellectual growth is a vital consideration in first school provision, and the necessary 'tool' subjects play a key part in the curriculum. Skills of 'oracy, literacy and numeracy' have wide-ranging implications for most aspects of development. Independent thinking and problem-solving are encouraged, while direct experience of the environment and the exploration of a variety of materials help children understand the world in which they live. Children's natural curiosity is a very strong motivating force, and the first school makes full use of it in planning learning situations, recognising the need to know and to achieve. A feeling of competence is an essential factor in the growth of independence and in the formation of a good self-picture, and every child should, at his own level, be encouraged to extend his knowledge and skills.

The importance of early learning

Much more attention has been given recently to the crucial nature of the early years, and at no time has there been a greater interest in these years on the part of both the general public and specialists in related fields. There is a large amount of ongoing research by psychologists, sociologists and paediatricians which is contributing important information to our understanding of the factors which influence children's learning and development. The rapid physical growth which takes place in the first years of life is paralleled by enormous steps forward in psychological development, and there are good reasons for believing that the learning acquired at this time is likely to be highly influential. An example of this amazingly rapid learning is the acquisition of language, where in the space of about three or four years most children have learned to use not only a wide vocabulary but most of the main structures of their own language. They have also learned to walk upright and unaided, to use finer movements for such skills as building with bricks or holding a pencil for drawing, to feed themselves, to listen to stories and repeat a few nursery rhymes, provided that their experience has not been restricted. (See Sheridan 1973, for a detailed account of developmental progress.)

The environment of the child

Although we are aware of the importance of the environment to general development, insufficient evidence is as yet available to indicate which aspects of the environment promote particular kinds of growth. Studies are at present being undertaken into a variety of topics, including the effect of the amount of space or the design of buildings, and the provision, kind and use of play materials and equipment. Interaction with adults, including verbal communication, and the value of structured programmes are areas of current interest.

Recognition of the importance of environmental factors in human development brings with it the acknowledgment that improving circumstances such as living conditions and welfare services should help in the achievement of potential, but it also implies a great responsibility for the school as an agency designed to intervene in the education of children. It then becomes more than ever necessary to look closely at what we mean by a 'good' or 'rich' environment.

The influence of home, family and community

At this point, however, it must be remembered that school is only one of the educative agencies in the life of the children, and the younger the child, the less influence school can exert, because of the relatively short time he spends there compared with the period spent at home or in its immediate neighbourhood. Barbara Tizard (1975) gives the timely reminder that

a child who attends a half-day nursery school from his third to his fifth birthday will have spent only about four per cent of the waking hours of the first five years of his life at school. Yet these are the years during which intellectual growth is most rapid.

Even when a child reaches the age of compulsory schooling he still spends most of his time with his family who, for this reason, and because of the strength of emotional bonds and his own great susceptibility to influence at this stage, remain dominant in passing on values and attitudes and preparing the child for entry into society outside the home. Thus the child's environment includes his experiences not only with the physical world but with people, and also his encounters with the structure of the society in which he lives. The child is especially sensitive to the situation provided by people as opposed to things, because of the reciprocal nature of their interaction – they can be relied upon to make some response! (Schaffer 1971.) And it is his experience with other people which helps him to make sense of his impressions of his surroundings, and to build up his own network of appropriate responses. Educational sociologists have been concerned with the influence of the family and home, particularly on attainment in school. Studies have brought out a series of factors such as parental interest and attitudes, values and language use, which have been thought to contribute to the differences in children's performance.

Moves towards extending contacts between home and school, and towards minimising the isolation of school from the wider community reflect this thinking, as does the introduction of special programmes (such as Project Headstart in the U.S.A.) designed to complement the learning which has already gone on, or to cater for special needs, notably in the field of language. The Plowden Committee's recommendations on the extension of pre-school education facilities have their roots in the insights gained from studies of home and community backgrounds, as well as the psychological work on individual learning and development. The first school by definition has a heavy responsibility for maintaining continuity of learning and promoting harmony between the dominant influences in a child's life. The first school teacher has to recognise that children do not develop in isolation from their cultural heritage.

Children's thinking

In the area of cognitive development, the picture given by Piaget and his associates remains central in describing the growth of children's thinking. Piaget shows that the child's understanding of his world is built up gradually through successive interactions with his environment. From the beginning he learns through his own activity, constructing his mental model through sensory impressions and motor patterns, through imagery and finally also through the use of language, which eventually serves to free him from immediate concrete reality. Piaget sees thought as 'internalised action', and an acceptance of this view supports the first school's provision of plenty of opportunity for direct experience in handling and manipulating materials.

Piaget's theory proposes that all children pass through a sequence of mental development just as they do in other kinds of development, and that this sequence is the same for all children. The first school stage includes major changes in children's thinking. When a child comes to school he is likely to be at the stage where he still views the world from his own position, and bases his conclusions on his perceptions. Thus he is frequently misled by appearances, and takes into account only one aspect of a situation. For example, a row of sweets spread apart seems to him to contain more sweets than a row in which the sweets are arranged closely, because it looks longer. Similarly, a piece of plasticine is believed to change in quantity when its shape is altered, because it appears thinner and therefore is considered to contain less, or longer and therefore more. Towards the end of the first school stage, at about seven or eight years of age, he begins to be able to make classifications, to see relationships and to retrace his actions mentally to his original starting-point. He has a greater realisation of cause and effect, and distinguishes more readily between reality and fantasy. In short, as he builds up a store of concepts about the world, it begins to make more sense to him. At this stage also he is becoming less 'egocentric' – that is, he is becoming more able to see from a point of view other than his own, both in his social interactions and in his encounters with the physical world. He still needs to be able to work out problems in concrete situations, however, dealing with real objects and experiences, if he is to develop operational thought, and for some children this will take much longer than for others.

Teachers therefore need to be aware of the child's level of understanding in various areas of work in order to plan for logical progression. A child would not be expected for instance to write down and work out a series of addition sums until he understood fully the number concepts involved. He would need to know that 'two' means the same whether it refers to two tables or two socks, or that a group of four objects remains constant however it is arranged. Matching the learning tasks we hope to promote with the child's present understanding is vital. If the task is too remote he will ignore it, and if it presents no challenge he will soon tire of it. Because the child is naturally curious, and learns through doing, at the first school stage successful approaches are largely based upon practical experience and activities which are relevant to his interests. Discussion and other oral work help him to clarify his ideas, and he is given valuable support by the use of materials and apparatus which enable him to tackle problems in a concrete way.

4 Developments in organisation and provision

As a result of increased understanding of children and of the desire for the education system to match their needs interesting developments have taken place both in the internal organisation of schools and in concentrating facilities and extra support in areas of special need. Programmes such as urban aid and the establishment of educational priority areas have been major attempts at maximising children's chances of reaching their potential.

Some of these changes in the internal organisation of schools have been attempts at incorporating into our larger primary schools the best traditions of intimate village schools. Among the best practices which have been included are the advantages of longer term contact with either one or more teachers; close involvement and liaison between older and younger children, and unstreamed classes, which have necessitated more individualised and flexible approaches towards the organisation of time and the curriculum. As each head teacher has autonomy there are many interpretations of these practices so it is important to remember that a common label may not indicate common practice.

Vertical grouping

Vertical, sometimes called family, grouping has been introduced into some infant and first schools. This grouping has children of different ages in the same class, perhaps five-, six- and seven-year-olds, or a modified form called transitional grouping with the fives and sixes or sixes and seven-year-olds together. First schools may have fives, sixes and younger sevens together with the older sevens, eights and nines grouped into other classes. Whatever age range mix a particular head teacher selects, it is usually based on a philosophy which aims at fostering social and academic growth. To parents who have never met this system before vertical grouping seems rather strange. They fear that the older children might be held back at the five-year-old level, for their own schooling probably took the form of whole-class teaching. For teachers, the problem is: where do you pitch your lesson if you do this? Do you aim at the 'average' child, leaving the least mature children to sink or swim? Or do you concentrate on the latter children? And what of the group who are most able? They may be very frustrated and will either become disruptive and demand attention or perhaps, worse still, become increasingly uninterested and lethargic. Vertical grouping, along with the introduction of the integrated day, has attempted to combat these problems.

What are the advantages of this form of grouping? In a well-run school they are numerous. Not the least advantage is that staff have a common denominator; no one teaches solely 'babies' or the 'top class'. Consequently kudos and problems are shared. No one can blame the previous teacher for not doing her job, or conversely leave major problems for the next teacher to tackle. All the teachers have the satisfaction of fostering a child's growth over a longer period. This extended responsibility and equality has the effect of welding a staff together with subsequent beneficial effects for the children. This additional security and collective positive response to children is a major feature. It is hoped that there will be several benefits for individual children:

1 Children and their parents will have two- or three-year contact with one teacher. (Vertical grouping presents a difficult problem for a head teacher who finds she has a 'weak' teacher. In order to help the children in that particular class she may have to give additional practical support.)

2 Small groups of new entrants will join established groups of

children who are already confident and competent in school routines and activities.

3 Children will have increased opportunities to work at their own pace. Five-year-olds will not be 'held back' at reception class level.

4 The group of children who are at the height of rapid skill acquisition will never be so large that the teacher cannot take full advantage of this enthusiasm. Large groups of these children in horizontally grouped classes can experience a great deal of frustration. Any extra attention given at this appropriate time can not be construed as unequal, for each child will in turn receive this support.

5 Children are more naturally able to share expertise, thereby practising and reinforcing their own skills. This does not imply for one moment that maturer and brighter children are used excessively as monitors or mini teachers, for the good teacher will see that they are also extended.

6 The mixed age range means that the maturer children, taking their cue from teacher attitudes, can do much to motivate, encourage and reassure others.

7 At a practical level there will be only a few children who will need assistance with dressing and tying shoelaces – any reception class teacher will appreciate how much valuable time can be wasted here.

8 Caring for others, the interchange of ideas and the stimulation towards achievement of any kind is more readily fostered.

9 Children can watch what others do, how they cope successfully or unsuccessfully with problems of sharing and co-operation and how they respond to stories and wide-ranging activities. They can see how others meet challenges. Children usually derive satisfaction and an additional sense of security by having this opportunity to view the continuum of development: 'this is what I used to be like when I was little and I shall be able to do that when I am older.'

10 If a teacher feels a child is not responding to her or that for various reasons they are incompatible, transfer to another class is comparatively easy within the system for all the groups contain parallel age ranges. Such transfers are rare for naturally a professional teacher will try to transcend personal feelings of animosity for a child. However, there are occasions when a teacher

finds a child so difficult or apathetic that she feels a move to another class would be beneficial for herself, the child and the class in general. Arrangements can be made with a willing colleague to wean a child gently from one group to another by letting him visit his new class over a period of time for various sessions and become gradually assimilated into it. A child is given a new chance to cope within a situation where he is not already labelled as 'naughty' by the children, and the opportunity to build a new relationship with a teacher who has not reached the end of her tether! Within traditional grouping exchange of children in this manner is rarely possible. In any case teachers are loth to admit problems of this nature as they feel it reflects some failure on their part, and indeed it may do so. But it would seem beneficial for everyone if such problems were made explicit, for a child who has acquired a derogatory label finds it difficult to shed. However delighted initially a child may be to be considered very naughty he may well find it a strain to live up to this image. This is why most teachers try to adhere to 'positive labels' reinforcing good behaviour and responses by praise. Conversely, if she is honest a teacher may recognise that her own reactions to a child are impeding his general development. It is particularly important in the vertically grouped situation to admit these problems – for otherwise a child may be with a teacher he is not compatible with for three years. A major staff meeting in May would be an appropriate occasion to discuss such difficulties so that a child could be prepared for a September move to another class.

Emotionally these groups, if well run (a necessary qualification whatever the system), are very supportive for children. The presence of various play opportunities and a wider range of equipment mean that periods of regression are readily catered for. Children under stress may seek the reassurance of home corners or easy apparatus without guilt feelings or fear of condemnation from their peers. Such regressions are not a waste of time, for they will frequently help a child to come to terms with problems more readily. They need to be viewed in realistic terms with regard to the time scale involved. One visitor to a vertically grouped class, who was obviously dubious of the desirability of the system, noted with considerable glee that a seven-year-old took out a very simple jigsaw and completed it. The process took only seconds. The visitor plainly saw it as far too easy a task. To the understanding teacher the child was seeking the reassurance of any undemanding activity. As adults we need to remind ourselves that there are so many things that young children cannot do that such moments of repetition are essential in achieving a well-rounded self concept, and need therefore to be viewed in perspective.

If the proposals for children to commence their infant school education at the beginning of the year after they are five are eventually implemented, nursery schools will experience the beneficial effects of the stimulus from maturer children who will move up into infant classes at a later stage. The problem of presenting them with enough challenge, however, will raise further questions about the content of the nursery school curriculum.

The devotees of vertical grouping find that the problems of extending maturer children are not insoluble and frequently devise opportunities for children to listen to more advanced stories and develop extended studies by teaming with a colleague. Adequate stimulation is always difficult and it would be foolish to postulate any method as a panacea. As we focus our attention more and more upon the desirability of our children growing into happy, secure and fulfilled adults, the best way of achieving this will continue to be debated.

The integrated day

In the most flexibly organised schools where approaches are based upon the understanding of individual maturational levels and needs, the integrated day was a natural development. This is an integrated approach to the organisation of individual time within a general framework. Irrelevant or false barriers between subjects have also disappeared.

Before embarking on any further discussion of the philosophies underlying the concept of the integrated day it might be appropriate to consider what one would see on entering a school using this approach.

It is difficult to describe a typical day for the tempo would vary from classroom to classroom. However the following description gives some indication of this approach:

On entering the school we observed small groups of children researching into animal habitats and the development of the railway system. A group was performing their own puppet play in the quadrangle. Other children, up and down corridors, were tending plants and animals, making models, typing stories, and a group listened to a taped story. Within the classroom areas children were constructing, painting, working in mathematical areas, reading, writing and adding work to class topics and interests. A group was gathered round their teacher making further plans for developing work from their morning's visit to the local church, another class listened to poetry. Everywhere children were reacting and interacting with people or materials. Yet apart from odd moments of frenzy there was a prevailing tranquillity and purposeful atmosphere.

How has this radical change in approach evolved and how is it possible to organise groups of thirty or more children to work in this manner? Let us look at some of the reasons which influenced the development of the integrated day.

The development of the integrated day

As attention moved towards developing the individual child's potential, so the day became more flexibly organised to accommodate individual differences. The integrated approach did not develop overnight. Twenty years ago most schools had strictly adhered-to timetables which had segments of twenty- or even only ten-minute intervals for 'subject' teaching. A typical timetable would have assembly, scripture, nature study, reading, copywriting, spelling, poetry, physical training, etc., and the whole class would receive one subject dose after another. Teachers merely forecasted their week's work and rarely evaluated it.

This approach was gradually recognised as inappropriate and so we began to divide the day into broader time bands. Usually the day began with free activities or play. The children had free choice for an hour and then they had to settle down to 'work'. Along with this free choice came a change in teachers' responses to children. Teachers increasingly said, 'That is lovely dear', whether it was 'lovely' or not. The teachers rarely interacted with the children during free activity periods, and were not involved in the ongoing work, merely making fleeting token responses, without extending the children's experience. Clearly this was a reaction against past rigidity. However, it was still incompatible with individual development for children were still having to stop one kind of work to start another. Many teachers recognised the absurdity of curtailing children's interests and concentration so abruptly and so the integrated day developed.

The integrated day involves a flexible approach to the organisation of individual and group time. Children have more possibility of working until they reach a natural stopping point. This learning 'climate' aims at encouraging the child's quality of thought, action and concentration. The work usually reflects this extension of opportunity for application and care. The teacher will look at longer time spans in a child's development and if, for example, he is becoming very competent and interested in a skill he will be given extended opportunities to reinforce this, for any periodic concentration upon reading, writing or mathematical skill would not be considered detrimental to eventual overall development. In fact most teachers would welcome such enthusiasm.

The term 'integrated day' also indicates the fusing of the curriculum. The sharp divisions between subjects have largely disappeared. For example, often a child's writing will involve drawing, reading, practising handwriting skills, his recall of experiences or imaginative inventions, the incidental teaching of phonics, as well as teacher-child interchanges. Similarly, brick building in a group may involve social skills, precise motor control, spatial skills, imaginative play, the practice and reinforcement of certain mathematical concepts, perhaps some later written work about the building and in the longer term a better understanding of map reading.

Although the integrated approach developed to maximise individual growth the teacher still groups the whole class together for various shared experiences. When necessary, too, she gathers a group together who, for example, need to be shown the mathematical shorthand of subtraction or division or who need additional language reinforcement.

Children have more choice within this framework but they are not left to drift, flit about or entirely depend upon their own initiative. Naturally a teacher cannot be everywhere. Longer sessions with certain individuals and small groups will mean reduced time for the other children, but even very short interactions can reassure a child by saying 'Yes I am noticing/caring about you too.' The good teacher gives guidance and encouragement to all the children. She expects perseverance and is less likely to accept initial efforts if she feels a child is capable of better work. Naturally the manner in which she does this would be positive and motivating. She tries to help the child see the potential in his work. For example she would challenge a child to think of some addition to his story by her questions about what the little boy in the picture was thinking about, going to do next, or hoping he would have for tea. She would also give extra guidance to children who are unable to cope with greater freedom in the planning of various aspects of their day. Fortunately the varying rhythms of the children's responses and behaviours (coupled with the variety of available activities) means that demands are not always simultaneous. A teacher's job would be impossible if they were!

Organising the classroom and its equipment

The integrated day will not function properly unless children are trained to take responsibility for cleaning, checking and clearing up their equipment. There will be clearly labelled and designated places for equipment and children would be expected for example to mop up any accidental spillage of water immediately in order to prevent the spread of what one class jokingly referred to as 'the great green Limpopo river'. Often attractive containers, accessible shelves and display units make tidying up pleasurable in itself.

Usually the teacher stipulates how many children can be in one area at a time. The home corner may accommodate three or four children, constructional work three and the painting area four and so on. Children learn these simple rules quickly and usually adhere to them.

These changes in approach have meant quite a development in the manufacture of equipment for the classroom. The teacher bases her choices upon criteria of flexibility of usage, durability, attractiveness, and whether the equipment is stimulating to the imagination. So, for example, she might buy two hundred small coloured cube bricks so that the children can build, sort, group, count, make rows of tens, find the cubic capacity of boxes rather than purchase something with a more limited range of uses.

Interpretations of the integrated day

In the infant school, as opposed to the nursery, some teachers would stipulate to the whole class various curriculum task requirements for the day; for example, 'I want you to do some news, reading and mathematics.' A reminder would be issued at the beginning of the afternoon session so that children would finish these tasks. This can be a limiting and somewhat dangerous approach, for there is a tendency for teachers to perpetuate the false dichotomy between work and play by saying get these tasks (work) done and then you can choose (play). This division of 'work' and 'play' is a regrettable concept and one that children with all their innate curiosity would never arrive at themselves. We do not wish them to think of reading and writing as chores to be done before they can play. Children can find all manner of things exciting. Often it is only the dullness of the approaches taken towards developing language and mathematical skills in our own early childhood which conditions us to think of them as 'work' to be suffered or tolerated. The dangers of this artificial division are exemplified by the bright six-year-old pottering along in a practical area at 9.20 in the morning who greeted another teacher with the words, 'I've done all my work for today, a bit of news, some number and reading and now I can play all day!'

Sometimes the integrated day is interpreted as the need to provide a series of tables for various aspects of the curriculum and then move the children at fixed intervals from one table to another. This puts the child back to square one, for he no longer has the opportunities for pursuing a problem with tenacity. Such a solution may look better, at a quick glance, than children sitting in serried ranks; but in reality it has just as many defects and frequently more. Unless there is a clear understanding by the children of the standards of commitment and behaviour expected by the teacher the integrated day can, in fact, *disintegrate* into a permissive slipshod affair which bewilders and dissatisfies children and teachers.

Teacher records

The ethos of a school with a smooth-running integrated day does much to challenge a child and foster purposeful activity and the meaningful development of skills. Under-achieving children and others with problems are more obvious to the teacher in such a system because she can view a child's behaviour in a variety of situations as he is no longer confined to a desk. She will keep records of the child's achievements (social as well as cognitive), his interesting comments, questions and successes as well as his difficulties. Nevertheless it is how the teacher reacts to this information, and her own observations, and what she does to extend, reinforce and reassure these children that is the hub of the matter.

Alongside records of plans concerned with general provisions and developments of class and group work the teacher often keeps a folder of a cross-section of a child's work so that she gradually develops a picture of his progress. Frequently she will give the head teacher and the child's parents a similar record, adding notes about the context of the work and its relevance to different aspects of the individual's development. It is useful if this can be a two-way process so that parents and teachers can build upon a child's direct experiences and mutually support and encourage him.

This need to evaluate our work in schools has been a major feature of the developments which have taken place during the last twenty years or so. To make effective records takes time and energy. There is no slick easy answer to record keeping. This relatively new and enormous demand upon teachers does pinpoint yet again the need for more help in the classroom. Many of the most relevant records are those which note day-to-day responses and discoveries. How is the busy teacher going to cope with all this motivating, responding, recording, evaluating, teaching and reassuring? Her role is continuously widening.

The mobility of the population causes problems for children and teachers. Children have to cope with the upheaval of moving house and then find themselves in a school whose policies are quite different from those of their previous school. A boy who is in the midst of learning to read by using the Initial Teaching Alphabet may, for instance, find himself the only child in the school doing so. Is his teacher prepared to learn or relearn how to use this medium? On the question of records there is no standardised policy for passing a child's records on to his new school. Indeed he may not even have any records — or those he has may not be especially helpful. Parents can try if they wish to inform their child's new teachers about his previous progress, but the serious lack as yet of any system causes many problems.

Open plan schools

As the infant school day became more flexibly organised the physical environment often came to be adapted to meet the newer interpretations of curricular needs. Teachers began to designate various areas of the room as places for particular activities. These areas were called number corners or painting corners and so on and were often accompanied by the appropriate written label. Tables, too, were used to display work or articles applicable to certain subject areas. The teachers strove to achieve different atmospheres in various areas of the room, often paying particular attention to attractive and quiet reading corners. The increased flexibility and widening of the curriculum in early childhood meant that great demands were made upon classrooms originally designed for much more formal approaches. The infant teachers, usually never lacking in ingenuity, began to divide the areas with small screens, cupboards, table groupings, book corners, sometimes indicating a change of emphasis and direction by the extra pieces of floor-covering they introduced. Rugs and carpet samples meant that children could work and read happily on the floor. As the children rarely used formal seating arrangements many of the tables and chairs became dispensable. In spite of all this skilful rearrangement the single classroom could hardly hold the variety of experiences the teachers wished to extend to their classes. Classrooms gradually started to creep out into the corridors. Sometimes interest tables would be placed in entrance halls so that more children could experience and enjoy them. Corners of cloakrooms housed woodwork benches. Valuable musical instruments, too expensive to be available in every class, were incorporated in corridor music corners. Every conceivable space was used. There were tranquil libraries, bustling shopping and market areas and 'special' dressing-up clothes, often housed near a long viewing mirror. So many interesting things were done within existing buildings.

Despite all these efforts it seemed desirable to make a more deliberate attempt to design new buildings that would help teachers achieve their aims and objectives. And so we saw the birth of open plan schools. Some of the early open plan schools were excellent and had a high degree of flexibility. Some of the more recent buildings may have pushed the concept too far, for the spaces are so vast and rectangular and lacking in areas for retreat that they pose many problems for staff and may be threatening to some small children. The best of these buildings seem to have captured the intimacy of the secure classroom and combined it with imaginative and attractive practical spaces. Although some local authorities liaise very closely with teachers about building design, in most areas there is not nearly enough consultation. It might be revealing to ask what the children think too, as some architecture students did with one class. Among the rather more flamboyant requests for chandeliers and settees were some revealing ones: more private lavatory facilities, foam rubber playgrounds (can you still feel the grit in your knees?), coat pegs at a safer height, and perhaps most poignant of all a quiet pl⁻ce to work undisturbed by visitors!

Schools for young children have in general gradually become less clinical, with more carpets, curtains and other soft furnishings. Walls, too, have come a long way from the standard brown and cream or green days. Textures, colours and more attractive furniture indicate the developing changes and emphases. The more domestic type of furniture may help to make the transition from home to school less traumatic for many children as well as lessening the sharp institutional atmosphere that many schools presented to parents.

Where open plan schools are a natural outcome of flexible organisation teachers gladly welcome the facilities and opportunities afforded by the building. What can happen though is that teachers with no desire to work in this way suddenly find themselves transferred to such schools. This usually occurs when a dilapidated building is being replaced. If the buildings are a half-way house between open and closed spaces the head teacher with her staff can gradually adapt, perhaps starting with a couple of teachers who would like to experiment with their organisation. Unfortunately, too, it does seem that some local authorities, and dare one suggest this has more to do with cost effectiveness than educational principles, build open plan schools in which practical areas have to serve as cloakrooms and corridors too. Using main thoroughfares in this way means constant hubbub and interruption – though, to be fair, many building designs do attempt to resolve these problems. Teachers will have to be prepared to be much more mobile to work successfully in these schools for children cannot be left merely 'occupied' in practical areas while the teacher stays in a self-designated tightly defined physical space. It is also essential that the design provides the teacher with an overall view of the areas, as she will find it disconcerting if she cannot see all the children.

Working in a team, whether it be in the nursery school or in a team-teaching situation in an open plan building, creates a number of related problems. It is ideal, in many ways, when all the adults are compatible or complementary. But day-to-day contact can breed irritation as well as admiration and much give and take will be necessary to overcome one's feelings of 'There she goes again, saying and doing the same old thing!' In the nursery school (and the first school which has nursery nurses and parent helpers) children will not make distinctions between the adults available. They will not say to themselves, 'I will ask the teacher about this matter because this concerns an intellectual/conceptual problem', or, 'I will ask for help with my dirty knees from the N.N.E.B.', but this very lack of distinction can give rise to conflict between the adults. The teacher will feel the need to be seen to exercise certain specific skills. A young teacher leading a team of mature highly experienced nursery nurses may not feel very sure of herself. It will take courage and patience to establish herself in these circumstances. A deliberate focus on forming effective co-operative partnerships may help.

There are many varieties of open plan school. Some have large spaces for 120 children to work in. Most incorporate the advantage of vertically-grouped classes as a wider age range of children will be mixing together in any case. In first schools there might be a nursery class for three, four and fives, with areas for fives with sixes, and sevens with eight-year-olds. Some schools have wider age range groupings but the concept of nursery, infant and junior education usually influences the groupings. Some head teachers decide to keep the children based in one place with one teacher for the teaching of basic skills, and for domestic reasons such as dinner money collection and register. This will be their 'home base'. Often the children will start and finish, both at lunchtime and teatime, with their home base teacher. She will be responsible for keeping records of this group of children's progress.

One advantage of open plan schools is that particular teaching skills and expertise can be more easily disseminated among groups of teachers. Imaginative and enthusiastic teachers can more readily and incidentally influence others. The teacher who is particularly skilled at handling children can help the general tranquillity of the area. The inexperienced teacher can gradually develop alongside her more experienced colleagues. Although it is advisable to have a clearly designated teacher for particular groups of children, all the children should benefit from the mix of personalities and might find another teacher that they relate to particularly well. Sometimes individual teachers are made responsible for certain aspects of the curriculum in which they have a special interest or expertise. Whatever method of teaming or co-operation is adopted, it is clear that with larger numbers of children in larger spaces the staff will need more opportunities to discuss the children's progress. Again, careful record keeping will be an essential part of this system. Unless a head teacher is very supportive a probationary teacher, while having the help of experienced colleagues, could easily feel overwhelmed by their ability to cope. Each teacher is more exposed to the others, and mistakes are made in professional public. This constitutes an enormous change for traditional teachers. Nevertheless, although open schools pose numerous problems, there are many successful ones running in the country. In an attempt to evaluate the successes and problems of management and organisation the Schools Council is currently running an inquiry.

Alongside these developments in organisation was the growing impulse to try to take positive steps to equalise opportunity. This desire was eventually translated into Educational Priority Areas and resulted in the development of various projects.

Educational Priority Areas

The Plowden Report recommended that various steps should be taken to discriminate in favour of disadvantaged children in areas of deprivation. Such areas tended to have common features: old dingy school buildings, large numbers of inexperienced teachers who after some teaching experience will move on to 'better' areas, a high immigrant population, poor housing combined with low wages and poverty. These areas are the first to suffer in times of economic recession. It was hoped that positive steps in the form of greater financial aid for equipment and buildings, additional payments for teachers, higher staffing ratios and expansion of general support would help to break the cycle of deprivation and give children a better chance to achieve greater educational equality. The Committee felt also that close links between parents and teachers were essential and that these areas were ideal places to set up community schools and to expand pre-school provision. It was hoped that education and social services would join forces to help raise local morale, parental interest and the children's performance.

To some extent such a policy is tackling the problem in isolation from its root causes – the serious general neglect of these areas in terms of work chances and possibilities of better things. Several of the U.S.A. Headstart programmes included consumer action services, giving advice on hire purchase and credit buying, and provided employment for the parents of children involved in the programmes, thus attempting to tackle problems at a more fundamental level. Several strands of support, economic, educational and social, would appear essential.

5 Roles and relationships: teacher, child and parent

The teacher

If we were asked to identify an element common to the many developments in early childhood education, the move towards greater flexibility would spring to mind. Whether we are considering kinds of provision available for the under-fives, or the organisation of space or time within a particular infant school, we are confronted with a much wider variety of possibilities than would have been admissible even twenty years ago. However, the demands upon the teacher of young children show a comparable diversity, and her role is by no means a simple one. Increasing knowledge of children's needs and of individual differences means that she must try to create a situation in which each child can feel secure and valued for himself. She will be ready to approve and to praise, and will ensure that every child has some success in order that he may build up a good self-picture. The close relationship between learning and emotion makes such an atmosphere vital if children are to be ready and eager to explore and to enjoy new experiences.

Children starting school

Many children on starting school have known only a small circle of family and friends, and may have had little opportunity to mix with others of their own age group. Here the example of mutual respect among the adults in school, and good relationships between teacher and pupil provide a basis for growing social skills. Children will gradually learn how to establish relationships with grown-ups and contemporaries through their experiences within the school community. They will be introduced to play situations in which co-operation is necessary – but when this breaks down they will be supported by the understanding of the teacher. They will meet other teachers, the cook, the caretaker and visitors to school, and they will be helped in this widening circle towards a greater awareness of the contributions which others make.

These aspects of the teacher's task assume great importance whatever the age of children under consideration, although the emphasis will be differently placed as the children mature and become more independent. Starting and changing school are periods when they are most vulnerable and in need of reassurance, and thus both nursery and infant teachers have a particular responsibility in that they lay the foundations of children's perception of school. If the school is seen as a welcoming interesting place, where the child is recognised as a unique person with his own special likes and dislikes, abilities and interests, he is likely to respond readily and settle more quickly into his new surroundings. The teacher will make sure that he is shown the lay-out of the building, or that part of it which he will use, and that he has a place in which to keep his personal possessions. He is always encouraged to bring something from home if he wishes to do so. He will be given his own space in the cloakroom, marked with his name or with a picture which he can recognise. Perhaps he will be invited to help the teacher in some task which he can easily perform, such as tidying the book corner or helping to arrange the interest table so that he feels that he is an accepted member of the group.

Inability to cope with such matters as washing hands, putting on coats or tying shoelaces can contribute to a child's failure to adjust happily to school life, especially where the teacher's expectations are high, and where the child has been given little chance to become independent of adults in these ways. The under-fives usually come into a situation which in its informality approaches as nearly as possible a family atmosphere, and they will be guided and helped towards self-sufficiency and confidence by the teacher and her team. Older children, especially where the school organisation is more formal, may need particularly sympathetic treatment if they are not to be made to feel conspicuous or inadequate. Some will have been prepared less well than others for the kind of responses which may be expected of them in school. For example, they may be unaccustomed to the social routines of meal times, and unless there has been discussion at home about playtime or assembly procedures they may be bewildered or afraid until through the adult's help and the example of their peer group they become familiar with them.

Values and standards

Children in the first school are also learning to see that certain rules and restrictions are necessary, in order that greater freedom may be enjoyed by the majority. They begin to be aware of values and standards, and of the existence and importance of other people's feelings. Here the attitude of the teacher towards her pupils and colleagues can provide one of many models with which children identify, and if she is consistent and rational in her treatment of day-to-day situations they come to understand the reasons for her decisions. Although a return to the authoritarian approach of the elementary schools of the last century would in no way be advocated, many educationists emphasise the 'standards' which it was the teacher's duty to support. Elvin (1969, p. 89) points out that

the teacher knew that he had a positive, not merely a permissive, function in the passing on of standards that society approved. The difficult thing to accept for those who were in the forefront of the fight against the old ways is that this last assertion is still true today and always will be. A too backward looking attitude, with warm thoughts of the victory that was won over the old way of inculcating standards, prevents our thinking hard enough about how society and the teacher can tackle this perennial problem in ways suited to our day.

He advocates that the teacher should have a picture of herself 'as acting positively, yet without the wrong authoritarian note which has happily almost gone', for this picture 'will communicate itself quite surely to the class and the school' (ibid., p. 102).

The learning environment

This positive role, with its implications of providing sufficient guidance, does not apply only in the area of values. Informal methods of teaching make great demands of the teacher. It is she who creates the learning environment, making choices based upon her aims and objectives. Similarly, although she places before the children the opportunity for making their own decisions, it is the teacher who opens up the range of possibilities. She has to be prepared to try a variety of methods, bearing in mind children's different ways of learning, and to alter her organisation or her programme to take account of immediate interests and individual needs. Yet flexibility and 'openness' call for a very carefully thought-out plan if each child's learning is to be catered for and each teacher's contribution to be respected.

For the teacher of the youngest children there has been a move towards more active participation in helping children to learn to think. The approaches of some compensatory programmes, although by no means universally applied or approved of in our schools, at least drew attention to the role of the adult in structuring learning situations relevant to children's experience. While still giving great weight to child-initiated activities, the teacher tries to strike a balance between these and the areas she thinks require specific emphasis. Children need help in ordering their learning, in seeing relationships and in making judgements, and language is a valuable tool. The teacher's provision of situations for varied language use and her own contribution through her techniques of questioning and discussion are being increasingly emphasised.

The teacher as a member of a team

The more widespread introduction of co-operative teaching situations and open plan schools has led to an extension of the teacher's role as a member of a team. In the nursery school, it has always been part of her function to act as guide to nursery nurses and students, and in the 'family' atmosphere she has worked alongside colleagues, sharing responsibilities, space and materials. The non-teaching staff ideally make distinctive contributions to the children's well-being, and the teacher has welcomed and valued these. A child who is having difficulty in adjusting to school will often make his first relationships with the cook in the shared setting of familiar tasks which maintain the link with home. At other times of stress, it may be the caretaker who provides solace and practical help, perhaps solving the problem of a broken toy or supplying the right material to complete a model. The same community principle underlies the work of the infant school, and with the increased employment of nursery nurses and ancillary helpers there is a wider circle of adults with whom the teacher works, and for whose duties she must plan. In this situation there is a great similarity now between the roles of the nursery and the infant teacher as initiators of ideas and leaders of a team. Frequently also the first school teacher will be responsible for advising and guiding students in training, and for planning programmes for secondary school pupils who spend time with young children as part of community service schemes or child care courses. Thus, not only must she be able to put her ideas into practice, but she has to communicate them effectively at different levels. A result of the more open nature of the infant school, and the 'team' situation, has been that the teacher is less tied to one particular classroom, instead moving freely between the various work areas which the children use. She thus tends to get to know a greater number of children and can make valuable contributions to the information about them which is gradually collected. The age range with which she deals is widened, and she extends her understanding beyond the single class boundaries. She therefore uses a greater variety of techniques, making different types of contact with the children as they develop (Gardner and Cass 1965).

Observation and evaluation

Working with different groups and individual children, especially where an integrated programme and co-operative teaching apply, has underlined the importance not only of a good knowledge of each child's background, capabilities and progress, but of keeping records which ensure that this knowledge is available in continuity to others concerned professionally with that child. More than ever the value of careful observation is emphasised, as the teacher is required to identify problems and to evaluate progress. Emotional stress is often identified through changes in a child's behaviour, and the teacher watches for examples of unusual aggression or tearfulness. Similarly she is alert to signs of difficulty in acquiring skills. She notices the child who handles jigsaw puzzles ineptly and is aware that he may need a lot of practice in manipulation and fine motor skills before he will succeed in forming letters easily.

The speed with which new materials, books and methods appear on the market makes it necessary to become adept at evaluating their worth if one is not to be beguiled by the transitory or trivial, but also on the other hand to be open-minded about innovation. Frequently the teacher adapts ideas and produces her own materials with the special needs of particular children in mind, and these are often the most successful. A readiness to make appropriate use of mechanical aids and an awareness of their possibilities is an additional facet of the task of the teacher which has grown rapidly in the last decade.

Children with special needs

Present thinking has included a consideration of the advantages of integrating children with handicaps into normal schools. Especially, the importance of nursery education for these children has been stressed, and it has become part of the teacher's role to work out the kind of provision which will best serve their special needs while enabling the group to function as a unit. Similarly, children from deprived homes may require help of a particular kind, and our increased knowledge of the implications of social deprivation enables us to cater for a wide variety of needs within the first school framework. An understanding of ethnic group differences has become highly relevant to first school teachers in many parts of the country, in order that they may appreciate the expectations and values of families of different cultural backgrounds, and work more closely with parents. These links with home, although always important, are vital where special needs exist.

Parents, their children, and relationships with teachers

Once on a train journey I met a mother and her two-year-old. We had a long conversation about many things and then discussed her son who was nearly eight and had recently been transferred to junior school. I asked how he was settling into his new school. She became quite upset and said that she had been to a parents' evening at which the teacher had said he was slow and not getting on well, and was backward with his maths. She said how surprised they were about this problem; her husband was a newsagent and apparently her son helped sort and number the papers and count the shop takings. They thought him to be 'quick'. I asked if she had told the teacher this but it was evident that it was not the kind of occasion when parents were permitted to inform teachers. She was despondent, anxious and unhappy. She could not really see the relevance of seeing the head teacher or trying to give the teacher a broader picture of her child.

What possible good could this negative one-way information achieve? Perhaps if the mother had felt less awkward and dictated to, the teacher could have heard about the boy's life at home and she might well have angled his mathematics work around newspaper distribution and costs. But there was no informal basis for this kind of rapport. It seemed the parents merely queued up on two evenings a year to have the opportunity to thank the teachers for their child's 'success' or to be blamed for his 'inadequacies'.

These attitudes of remoteness seem extraordinary. Parents are still all too often expected to be subservient and grateful recipients of the sometimes indifferent education offered to their children. Teachers continue to dole out platitudes. It would be unrealistic to convey the impression that parent–teacher liaison is developing everywhere. Not all teachers or parents see the necessity for or ad-

vantages of such co-operation and it will clearly take time to overcome the view of school as entirely separate from the community.
Many parents – and teachers – would not consider that the school
had a role in the child's emotional upbringing – in helping him to
become a happy, secure, fulfilled adult. Some middle class parents,
moreover, may be perceived as too interfering and as attempting to
dominate school policy without having the necessary expertise.
Teachers complain that some of their voluntary parent helpers take
more looking after than the children! And parents resent the feeling
that they are 'used', without being allowed to have a real voice in
their child's schooling. So it would be foolish to consider the picture
as all rosy. Teachers are anxious that the professional role of the
teacher be safeguarded, feeling understandably that it would be a
serious mistake if it were thought that all or any kinds of teaching
could be done without professional training for the job. The case for
the dovetailing of nursery and infant education has been discussed
already; the case for the greater dovetailing of upbringing (in the
home) and education (in the school) is equally strong. To strike a
more positive note, however, there have been some substantial
strides in the area of co-operation between parents and teachers. In
many schools there have been effective partnerships which help to
foster children's developmental growth. These good practices have
stemmed from the realisation that a child must be viewed as a whole
person and that it would be absurd to work in isolation from, and
without regard to, the major influence in their lives – their homes and
families. It seems appropriate to discuss some of these developments,
first by looking at nursery schools, starting school and then considering some of the planned and informal meetings.

1 The nursery school

From the earliest days of nursery education there have been close
links between parents and teachers. These have stemmed quite
naturally from the fact that parents need to go into the school to help
deliver, de-boot, de-coat and collect their young children. Much two-
way information was gleaned in this manner. In the 1920s and

onwards many nursery schools had Mothers' Clubs where problems could be aired and shared. Opportunities arose, particularly in working class areas, for mutual self help. The need for this kind of inter-group support is even greater today for we have many more instances of young mothers being geographically isolated from their extended families, while grandmothers, even if they are nearby, may well have jobs. As patterns of family life have changed drastically since the fifties, so schools and teachers need to take cognisance of these changes and modify their approaches.

Most of the ways of developing good relationships and the underlying principles that are discussed are appropriate for all the stages of early childhood education.

2   Entry to school

One smiles when one of the major claims for the necessity for nursery education is that it eases entry into the infant school. There will be a beginning whenever it is and it could be much more traumatic at the tender age of three. Frequently the first occasion a child enters school is when his name is put on the admissions list. This first meeting is vital; it will set the tone for subsequent rapport, or lack of it. The head teacher usually deals with this stage. If she lays great stress on the trappings of her authority by having a big official barrier desk and 'Head teacher' emblazoned on her door and adopts an equally official tone, the idea of the inaccessibility of the profession will be reinforced. If she is warm, friendly and keeps officialdom to a minimum this must help to ease the situation. Nursery schools and many infant schools invite parents and their children who will shortly start school to a series of short meetings which perform a variety of functions:

1   General school information can be quickly disseminated
2   Such information can also be handed out in booklet form – some schools and local authorities have delightful introductory booklets, some illustrated so that parents can share certain aspects with their children
3   Parents of new children can meet one another

4 Parents and children can be introduced to the class teacher
5 Parents and children can view the school and become familiar with its layout facilities
6 Arrangements can be made for the children to come with their parents, or a parent, for short periods on at least three or four further occasions before starting school
7 The need for initial part-time attendance can be discussed. This applies to both nursery and infant schools
8 The desirability of children going home for lunch until they become quite settled can be emphasised

It is preferable that at least some of these meetings take place when the school is in session. It can create problems, however, if all the new reception class children and their parents arrive to see a class teacher while she is looking after her class. This, of course, is another reason for advocating vertical grouping as there would never be a large number of new entrants to a group at any one time. Such meetings need careful organisation if they are really to do the job which is intended. Many nursery schools encourage mothers to stay with their children for at least the first week in school – and will let them know that this is desirable in advance. Other head teachers suggest that parents try to bring their child to visit the school on at least twelve occasions before starting school.

3   Planned programmes

In schools where the teachers are anxious to foster good relationships between themselves and parents, a number of different approaches are possible. The 'mix' of these approaches will depend upon the area and the particular needs of the community. The planned approaches may include evenings devoted to:

1 Lectures by visiting speakers and resident staff on aspects of the curriculum and child development
2 Demonstration of materials
3 Exhibition of children's work, perhaps based on various aspects

of the curriculum, for example mathematics work or children's developmental growth illustrated by their creative work

4 Talks by specialists in related fields: the librarian, school doctor, speech therapist

5 Hired films of specific and general interest; video tapes, slides and films of ongoing school activities (these are frequently the most popular as parents have the opportunity of seeing their children at work)

6 Opportunities for fathers and mothers to visit classrooms and talk to their child's teacher

7 Social activities such as coffee evenings, dances and travel talks

8 Fund-raising events such as the proverbial 'jungle' sale (as young children call jumbles), bring and buy

9 Displays and sales of toys and books, perhaps before Christmas so that parents can see the excellent materials which are available

10 Daytime occasions for meeting might include opportunities for parents, or grandparents, and younger children to visit school for assemblies, stories, concerts and traditional festivals

11 Coffee mornings, as well as being social gatherings, can be times when the children can be hosts to their parents: they may be involved at a variety of levels, from preparing and serving food to guiding their guests around the school and explaining their group and individual work

4 Informal approaches

These are essentially unplanned, but are frequently the times when a teacher can be of most help, by listening sympathetically when parents most need it. Some nursery schools devote the first half-hour of the morning session principally to the parents, recognising that this kind of involvement, although not always directly concerned with the immediate needs of the children, is supportive in the longer term to the whole family. To facilitate the growth of this informal interaction more schools incorporate parents' rooms in their buildings. Here parents can relax, exchange information about their children, develop the companionship which can be difficult to foster in some communities, for example in high rise tower blocks, and help with various domestic chores in the classroom. Mothers can also discuss any home problems which may be affecting their child.

The teacher's role will be complex. She will be required to give specific detailed information as an authority on the educational, social and physical needs of children, but she will also need to listen with infinite care to the equally specific and detailed information the parent has about her child.

5 Parental involvement in schools

In the past two decades more and more deliberate attempts have been made at harnessing the valuable practical help parents can give to schools. Frequently this direct involvement has become a burning issue in the teachers' unions. In early childhood education where the necessity for extra listening ears and pairs of hands has been a high priority such help has been largely welcomed with open arms. It takes a variety of forms. Some head teachers encourage mothers (for it is usually mothers who have the opportunity to help) to perform many of the menial tasks associated with the day-to-day provision and maintenance of equipment in the first schools. This can be un-popular, for no young isolated mother will consistently want to exchange one round of domestic tasks for another. So perhaps the cutting, pasting, repairing, washing and sewing can be interspersed with opportunities for closer contact with children and teachers. Of course if the parent covers books in the corner of a classroom this will be an additional interest for children as well as providing someone else to talk to. The parent, too, will be able to observe incidentally the teacher's interaction with the children.

Some parents will be able to offer their special expertise. They can carry out activities with small groups of children such as cooking, simple sewing, laundry and gardening work that teachers find extremely difficult to cope with as they usually require close adult–child contact for longish periods. Fathers may be able to work in school time repairing toys and making animal cages, working with small groups of children, perhaps doing woodwork, or telling a story to a small group. They can come and talk about their jobs. Better still, very small groups of children with the help of parents might visit a father's work place. A nursery teacher took groups of five children with various helpers to the local steel works where many fathers worked. The resulting benefits for the children and the fathers quite amazed her, for the special father–child bond seemed to be considerably reinforced. More schools seem to be involving 'foster' grandmothers in various activities. There is no doubt there can be an especially close rapport between the old and very young, but perhaps the encounters need to be of short duration as sometimes the old, unless they are used to the persistent demands of young children, can only tolerate them in small doses.

All parents should be encouraged to observe their children at work in school. Some will not be able to involve themselves in regular commitments, and it is particularly useful in these cases if fixed arrangements can be made for them to see the school functioning. In some schools this has been successfully achieved by giving parents considerable choice of times, but keeping the numbers involved on any occasion very small. As these occasions are essentially observations of usual classroom practice the teacher is fully occupied and wishes the children to work as normally as possible. The children, if adequately briefed, usually respond very well to keeping to their normal programme, provided that they know that they have other opportunities for talking about their work to their parents.

6   Home-visiting teachers

As more and more women work and as society imposes greater pressures on women there are, as there have always been in the past, many parents who for a variety of reasons do not have close contact with the people who have educational responsibility for their children. In some countries, notably Russia, class teachers are expected to visit their pupils' parents at least once a year. It is only in recent years that schools have begun to extend their boundaries in this way. There is by no means a consensus of opinion in this matter.

However, some local authorities appoint home/school liaison teachers, sometimes supported by a nursery nurse whose job is to liaise with a school or group of schools and parents. They will adapt their role to the particular needs of their community. In areas with high proportions of other ethnic groups a principal feature of their job might be to encourage mothers to learn English. They may need to introduce to parents the idea that play materials are necessary (when in their native country – say India or the West Indies – with plenty of sunshine and opportunities for outdoor play, they may not have seemed to be). Such teachers have to be especially sympathetic and non-authoritarian if they are to perform their function well. They can visit forthcoming entrants to school and generally inform parents of the school facilities and help them to prepare their child for school. Home/school liaison teachers can help a class teacher and parents adjust their approaches to a child by visiting his home and explaining any difficulties. As teachers we do not always know a child's background and can make gross errors in our assumptions about the reasons for his behaviour. Such visits can help identify possible sources of problems so that positive steps can be taken to help parents, children and teachers.

Above all the teacher's role in relation to the parents of the children she teaches is to work towards providing the best possible educationally and emotionally supportive environment for these children. Close communication between parent and teacher about such matters as the arrival of a new baby, a death or unhappy major or minor disruption in the family means that a teacher can anticipate possible problems and help the distressed child. For example, a teacher might talk generally about babies and make the child with a new baby in his family experience personal kudos within the group. She can more readily understand and deal with sudden aggressive behaviour and generally support the child. Parents need to feel especially secure that their confidences will remain as such. The teacher must be seen to be scrupulously fair in her dealings with parents. She will need to recognise the special problems of single-parent families, perhaps introducing the parent to mothers who can help by taking the children along to school or by putting them in touch with the Gingerbread Group (a group formed by single-parent families to provide mutual help) and by giving extra support to the parent and children during stressful periods. Many parents face extreme problems during their children's early years, but few are not glad to see a teacher's intense interest in, and knowledge of, their children. Most parents are considerably less in awe of teachers than they were twenty years ago. Unfortunately many of the parents least likely to come to school have experienced failure and rejection in their own education. Every effort must be made to draw them into the community of the school because there they will have the opportunity of receiving considerable reinforcement through their own child's success, and of seeing, often to their great surprise, how much concern and interest many teachers have for individual children. In this way inroads can be made towards breaking depressing cycles of 'failure'. Some schools ask other parents to help by approaching these families and accompanying them on their visits to the school.

The teacher will need to be well-informed and able to articulate the reasons for her various educational decisions. She receives far more support from the media than in the recent past, for many excellent informative programmes about child development are shown on television and increasingly women's magazines run features about the education of children. Many schools have small resources of books, journals, magazines and colour supplements for parents to borrow. Generally the public is better informed and this increasing knowledge, linked with teachers' greater understanding and acceptance of the need to listen and co-operate with parents, provides a supportive foundation for early childhood education. Once this concept of team work is established the ultimate benefits for children are potentially enormous.

PART II

Aspects of the curriculum

This section is concerned with the kinds of educational experiences which are presented to children in school. Planning the development of experiences for young children is a complex task and indeed there are still those who consider that a 'curriculum', either written or implicit, is inappropriate during these early stages. However, there is growing agreement that we need to identify 'good' practices and to classify our aims and objectives and their consequent influences upon the curriculum. Many factors are important in this planning, and there are at least ten main elements influencing its development. These include:

1 Ways in which the content and approach feed physical, social, emotional, aesthetic and moral, as well as intellectual development

2 The need to cater for individual differences, which ought to include a thorough examination of the varying needs and developmental rates of boys and girls

3 The need to develop language skills and mathematical concepts

4 The development of the ability to solve problems and concentrate upon wide-ranging tasks and experiences

5 The desirability of including structured programmes for certain aspects of the curriculum: the sequential content of these programmes may help children with special needs

6 The need for flexibility and manoeuvrability within the planning structure, to allow a teacher to expand child-initiated discovery

7 (a) The children's need for continuous feedback and reinforcement

(b) The teacher's need for feedback as evidenced by the children's responses and the teacher's records of their progress

8 Time for reflection and recall by the child: what Britton (1970) has called the spectator role

9 The essential development of a positive self concept, with its implications for the provision of opportunities for role and dramatic play and other forms of self-expression

10 The relevance of the subject area to different aspects of development

This list demonstrates the complexity of the task and the many factors which have to be considered when we plan and develop the curriculum. As the developments in organisation have demonstrated, greater flexibility in the use of time and space, alongside the integration of subjects, has reflected the growing concern for relevance and appropriateness in the curriculum for the individual child as well as the class.

Although it has been stressed that this approach is hardly compatible with major divisions between subjects the teacher will need to express her ideas in some convenient form of categorisation. It could be 'being, making and finding out' or almost 'doing, thinking and reflecting' but for the purposes of this book the experiences have been divided into these broad areas: language skills, developing play experiences, using the environment, and a collection of experiences which could be broadly classified as 'aesthetic'. The development of language skills is considered of prime importance and therefore is discussed first. Play, environmental and aesthetic experiences are discussed for their intrinsic value, and for the ways in which they provide additional relevant support towards developing skills.

6 Language skills

The anxiety of most parents that their children should be able to read expresses itself in a number of ways, and one frequently hears the criticism that departure from more traditional methods of teaching has brought with it a lack of concern for the basic skills of literacy. A survey undertaken for the Bullock Committee, however, 'gives no evidence of a large body of teachers committed to the rejection of basic skills and not caring who knows it' (Bullock Report 1975, para. 1.8). On the contrary, in schools where much of the most interesting practice goes on there is deep-rooted commitment to the promotion of language skills in all their aspects. It is rather in the extension of our ideas of what reading and writing entail that one of the major changes in present-day approaches lies, a view confirmed by Saunders (1976) in his volume in this series.

The importance of spoken language

The Plowden Report (Central Advisory Council for Education (England) 1967), in emphasising the 'central role' of spoken language in learning (para. 53), draws attention both to the importance of speech as the basis of early reading and writing and to the need for a rich background of experience from which speech can develop. A child who has a poor background both of language and experience is likely to find learning to read difficult. It is with these points in mind that the first school makes its provision. As children go about their various tasks, they are encouraged to talk. This encouragement of conversation is not just a matter of permissiveness – although this is part of its function also – but is essential to a teaching policy founded upon an understanding of the vital contribution made by speech to a child's general development. The availability of more sophisticated recording apparatus and techniques has enabled both research workers and practising teachers to collect far more accurate and frequent samples of children talking, and an analysis of such samples can give valuable insights into the purposes which language serves. At the nursery school stage, children playing together use speech to maintain contact with each other, although often their conversation runs on parallel lines as if they are not really interacting, but are content to play companionably side by side. The running commentary which is characteristic of the talk of children at this stage helps them to control their activities, probably by drawing their attention more closely to what they are doing. Through interchanges with others, they learn more about their reactions and feelings, begin to adapt to their audience and learn to influence other people's responses. When four-year old Jane, having made up her mind which doll's bed she wants to use, says to her companion persuasively, 'You have the little cot, Pat, and I'll have the bed', this is just what she is trying to do. She shows an awareness that some reasonable arrangement might be made which would satisfy Pat and at the same time bring about the outcome she herself wants. Some children will be able even at this early stage to use language to draw upon and discuss past events in order to sustain an argument and to express relationships. This demands highly complex organisation. Joan Tough gives a detailed and illuminating account of the functions of children's language, including transcripts of the recorded speech of children at play, in the second chapter of her book (Tough 1973), which indicates the complex level of usage which is possible by the time a child enters school.

Pre-school experience

Although by three years of age most children can cope quite competently with speech for purposes such as making their wants known and attracting attention, there are wide individual differences in both the amount of language used and in its variety. Some of these are matters of personality, for in order to engage in conversation, one must be willing to do so. A shy child may find it very difficult to communicate, especially in a strange situation, until he feels secure and has established relationships. Some are able to talk to other children more readily than to adults, some are more at ease with grown-ups and some are naturally less outgoing. In addition, however, there are likely to be extensive variations in the language experience children have had in their early years. It is not only that some may not have been sufficiently exposed to language. They may not have encountered the same number and kinds of uses to which it may be put. It is important that the teacher is aware of this, and that while accepting the children's language and recognising its value, she has a very clear idea of what she can do to extend it.

The teacher's part

So far we seem to have considered mainly children talking to each other, yet although this fulfils many essential functions it is language contact with understanding adults which makes for progress. When the child enters school he needs situations in which he can use language for comparing and analysing, describing and explaining, and a teacher available to help him at appropriate moments. The use of the tape-recorder has given many of us an entirely new view of the ways in which we talk to children. So often it appears that we as teachers do most of the talking, and by the questions we ask frequently inhibit further conversation! Consequently many teachers have taken a fresh look at their techniques of explaining and questioning, trying to phrase what they say in such a way that the child is encouraged to continue talking, to seek answers to problems and to try out his ideas, however tentatively.

Striking a balance between helpful promoting and interference can be a major problem. A five-year-old boy was talking to his teacher about a picture in a book he was looking through. He describes the scene:

MARTIN This is a man's house that's on fire, and he's gone to ring the police and the fire engine to come up in the 'phone box, and he's got grey trousers . . . and he's got a white shirt and there's white there and there.

TEACHER What do you think the man is feeling? How do you think he feels?

MARTIN Upset because his house is on fire because the house cost a lot of money.

TEACHER What would you think he's saying?

MARTIN He's saying 'Can I have the fire engine, the fire brigade?'

TEACHER And he's probably saying 'Please will you send . . .'

MARTIN The police. Why do they send the police too?

TEACHER I wonder – what do you think they send them for?

MARTIN Talk to them about something. I don't know what they talk to them about.

TEACHER Perhaps to make a report on what's going on, and perhaps to see if anyone happens to get . . .

MARTIN Hurt, and 'phone the ambulance.

TEACHER What would the ambulance do?

MARTIN They would take them to hospital and they would examine them and see if they was all right.

As this episode shows, it is not as easy as it may appear to make the right comment or ask an appropriate question at the opportune moment. The conversation can take unexpected turns which are sometimes disconcerting. On the other hand these may reveal a child's lack of understanding or ability to verbalise, or may show up a hitherto unrecognised maturity.

Teachers have become more aware of the need to give a child time before they intervene, to accept his contributions readily and to respond to his advances. They are more alert to the dangers of implying that his speech is in some way inferior, and of constantly correcting him, or insisting upon the conventions of 'please' and 'thank you' when he is eager to tell them about something of vital importance to him. In the above transcript, Martin says '. . . and see if they was all right.' To point out his grammatical error would have been out of place here, for his attention was on the content of his conversation. The teacher's own speech, and the language of stories will act as models, and there will be appropriate times when she feels it would be right to help him incidentally or indirectly. Sometimes it seems natural quietly to repeat the child's phrase in amended form — 'Yes, to see if they were all right' — but not at a time when it would interrupt the talk.

Language experience in school

(a) A climate for growth The first essential is to create a climate in which the child wants to communicate with others, and feels free to do so. It is essential too that he has something which he wants to talk about, and later to write about. A school which gives a warm, welcoming impression, where the atmosphere is home-like and each child is made to feel that he matters is likely to be far more successful than that which presents a front of bleak anonymity. This is often partly achieved by thoughtful organisation of space, so that, for example, large forbidding areas are broken down into smaller units, but the relationships which exist within the school are a crucial factor. '. . . it is the particular kind of shared life created by all those who work together in a school which determines how language will be used by teachers and pupils' (Rosen and Rosen 1973, p. 21).

Under the heading of language skills must be considered the related aspects of speaking, listening, writing and reading, and the good language environment will provide opportunities for all of these throughout the day as a matter of course. Both at nursery and infant school level, play provides an ideal setting for interacting through language. Many teachers are ingenious in selecting experiences to give children the opportunity to use words familiar to them through their home and family life. Children will be encouraged to extend vocabulary appropriate to the concept being employed. For example, in water-play children learn that things float or sink, that they can fill and empty containers, can use funnels, tubing, sieves. Sand is wet, or dry and powdery, dough is sticky. They learn the vocabulary of colours, shapes and textures, and the frequently-changed displays initiated by the teacher give rise to much exploration and talking. In one school the production of a 'shiny corner' came appropriately towards Christmas time, and it seemed that contributions appeared from all sides. The teacher linked nursery rhymes and songs with the visual experience. The little star twinkled more brightly, and the nut-tree's silver nutmeg and golden pear took on new meaning as the words were savoured alongside the collection of silver and golden objects.

(b) Stories and poems   The child who is accustomed to hearing stories read and told comes to school with a great advantage, for he has begun to appreciate the pleasure which words bring. Other children need a lot of practice before they can listen to and enjoy stories, but it is a major part of the teacher's task to ensure that they can all have this opportunity. There is a place for both reading and telling and much to be said in favour of each, for in some ways they serve different if complementary purposes. The intimate atmosphere of the small group to whom an adult is telling a story is highly conducive to learning, and perhaps this is less easily achieved by reading, but the skilled teacher becomes adept at 'telling' while still referring the children to the book for special purposes. This introduces children to the notion that print holds interesting information and teaches them how books should be treated, thus pointing the way towards the beginnings of reading. For some children early experience of looking at picture books with their mother will have taught them to appreciate books long before they reach school age, but others come to school quite unfamiliar with the left-to-right direction of print and 'beginning at the beginning'.

Children's love of rhythm and of humour can be satisfied through the teacher's choice of poems and stories, and the type of story which uses repetition and gives a chance for participation is usually successful. Here, listening and talking come together. Some teachers use puppets, through which the shy child will often communicate, and stories such as 'The Little Red Hen' lend themselves particularly to this treatment. Waiting for the moment to say 'Not I' when one is playing the cat's role demands concentration and understanding of a high degree. It is important that the language of the stories is not too simple. Children can, if the context helps to supply the meaning, appreciate much more subtle choice of words than those supplied in the average reader from a graded scheme. Beatrix Potter's stories are rich in such language usage, and many children have delighted in the 'soporific' effect of too much lettuce upon the Flopsy Bunnies! Because listening to stories enriches language use, gives opportunity for identifying with characters and learning how others feel, releases tensions and enlarges experience of the world, it seems a great pity that not every teacher places a high priority on reading aloud to children far beyond the first school stage.

(c) The use of books   The introduction of books at the appropriate time, accompanied by the adult's suggestions and discussion, can make a significant contribution to extending language as well as play experiences and interests. For example, a child may want to identify a bird he has seen in the garden or to find out exactly how his motorway bridge should look. The teacher too will refer to books for detailed information when children's questions make it obvious that they need to find out more fully about a particular subject, and this can provide another shared experience leading to greater understanding of why we read. At first, pictures and diagrams will provide the clues for children, supported by discussion, but later they will read for themselves. The teacher's own pleasure in books, and the way she looks after them, will largely determine the children's reactions, just as the way in which the adults in school talk to one another and to the children will affect the latters' approach.

An environment which is intended to promote language skills must be well provided with books, and many schools choose to spend a substantial proportion of their allocation of money on these. Local libraries provide an invaluable and greatly appreciated loan service, and often groups of children are welcomed in the library where they become familiar with the organisation and can select and read at leisure. Some children's librarians also provide story sessions and these are extremely popular. For the younger children, the sheer size of the establishment and the number of books can be overwhelming, and they often gain most from the smaller displays in their own room or teaching area. It is usual, therefore, to see in the first school a number of 'book corners' or reading areas in which the teacher creates a situation which is manageable for the child. Attractive displays of carefully selected books, with illustrations, encourage children to go and read at odd minutes during the day, and such areas are rarely empty. Sometimes children's attention will be focused on a particular interest for which the teacher can be ready. After the visit of a mounted policeman it is to be anticipated that children will want to see books about horses and the police force! At the same time, individual needs must be considered. Older children who can read fluently for themselves will of course begin to refer more to books for information, and they use this knowledge, coupled with that gained through first-hand experience, in their own writing on either individual or group topics. Often it has been found useful to introduce writing and drawing materials into the book corner, because children frequently want to record immediately, in some form, the ideas which their reading has initiated.

A well-planned library will include books of both fact and fiction. Many children are led to a lifelong appreciation of literature through being sensitively introduced to it by the teacher. Some older children will be beginning to enjoy longer books, and one useful technique is to read aloud a representative selection from a book which is then prominently placed in the library area for children to continue for themselves if they wish. Children should have the opportunity to take books home, and will be encouraged to discuss their reading with parents and teachers. Perhaps it has not always been sufficiently realised that a shared interest of this kind, which brings together home and school, has great educational significance.

(d) Talking Children who have been involved in a variety of experiences will normally be eager to record or re-live some of these, first through talking, drawing or painting and later through writing. It is important however that they are given time to absorb their experiences, and the once-popular 'news time' when a whole class was expected to contribute items of news in turn, is now generally regarded as an artificial and possibly inhibiting situation. Not all children are ready to talk about every experience, and certainly not to order. Nowadays more informal groups are usual and children discuss and share matters which hold real interest for them as they are

working or when the occasion arises. As they develop, they gain from talking to each other and often use language in quite complex ways for planning ahead, exchanging ideas or developing arguments. They will, for example, discuss the next move in building a boat from crates and boxes, and give reasons for their particular choice of method or material. Time is made available for individual conversations as well as group discussion between child and adult, and here the nursery nurse and teacher's aide have a valuable part to play. Through her questions, suggestions and general participation the adult helps the child to think about his experiences, and to make sense of them through language. At the same time, the teacher will observe closely in order to learn which aspects of his language development require special attention. Some children, for example, will need a great deal of experience in order to acquire a vocabulary of colour or size, and she will ensure that she discusses particular children's problems with her team so that they may work towards common goals.

(e) Language programmes Concern for those children whose background of experience is narrow has led to research and experiment into possible ways of providing specific teaching to complement the normal school programme. There have been a number of attempts in the U.S.A., including that of Bereiter and Engelmann (1966), to introduce highly structured programmes of instruction in situations usually closely controlled by the adult, but there are elements of inflexibility in these which do not fit in with the traditions of British early childhood education. In this country recent work involving the use of language development programmes has been carried out for example as part of the Schools Council Project in Compensatory Education and of the N.F.E.R. Pre-school Project in which the Peabody Language Development Kit (Dunn and Smith 1964) was used in a modified form. The whole question of the introduction of structured programmes and language kits is a matter of controversy, and certainly many teachers have not been happy about the restrictive nature of some of these. It is important however that the teacher should be aware of the many different facets of language use, and 'structured' programmes have at least drawn our attention

to elements which might be overlooked – such as using language for explaining and comparing, and for giving instructions. The Bullock Report (para. 5.26) sees the value of 'guides of one kind or another to help the teacher to develop the child's language', and suggests that

there is also a place for programmes of a kind appropriate for English schools; they have a value in alerting the teacher to particular language needs, and they help her ensure *every* child's active involvement in small group work. But the guide should be a support for the teacher's initiative, not a substitute for it; and the programme should be an integral part of the rich environment she creates as a source of constant stimulus to language.

(f) Focusing upon a reading environment Upon foundations of this kind, the first school builds the skills of reading and writing. Many children will be used to seeing adults at home reading books and newspapers, and writing letters and lists, and for these the written word will be part of their normal background. It is thus easier for them to make the vital link between written symbols and meaning. Their curiosity includes the printed word. 'What does that say?' is a frequent question which merits a satisfying answer. Others, although exposed to print in the form of street names, advertisements and traffic signs, may not see its purpose if their attention has not been drawn to it by adults. The environment of the school is designed to help children understand that the printed word can be interpreted into speech which conveys meaning. Children are introduced at an early stage to the written form of their own names, so that they can identify their possessions, and they are proud to be able to 'read' these. The teacher talks to them about new additions to the domestic play area, or the nature table, and writes captions in sentence form, sometimes at the children's dictation, which she then reads back to them. Their drawings, paintings and models are discussed, and these too have their interesting written descriptions to be talked about and read. Sometimes a series of illustrations by the children are made into a 'wall story' which tells a sequence of events; others are used to produce books of an individual child's work, or that of a group pursuing a particular interest. These books then become a part of the library collection, and children take great pleasure in looking at the

pictures and 'reading' with the teacher the story which accompanies them.

Progress towards reading and writing

(a) Using language experience   In the first school the total language environment linked with direct experience is planned to motivate children to want to read and write because they can see the purpose and relevance of this means of communicating. From suggesting the words they would like the teacher to write to explain their pictures, they progress first to copying and then to producing their own sentences. These early efforts, which link reading and writing, are good indications of progress, and are particularly valuable as records for the teacher. They may be used to help in explaining to parents that their children are in fact learning to read, for many become extremely anxious if they have not yet begun to work their way through a graded series of books, and would be happy to have evidence in the form of a personal record which they and the child can read together.

(b) Developing reading skills   It is important that, as far as possible, parents and teachers do not communicate to children their anxiety about reading progress. Children very quickly sense the feelings of those who are close to them, and if they too become over-anxious their learning can be impeded. Perhaps the past controversy about 'reading readiness' has been responsible for many of the misgivings felt concerning the teaching of reading. It is no longer held that readiness to learn to read depends almost entirely upon reaching a particular stage of development. Nor is it now suggested that simply to expose a child to a good learning environment will necessarily ensure that he learns to read. Since reading is a learned skill, we must accept that teaching will be needed. Of course certain abilities are pre-requisite, and the teacher sees that each child is given the experiences he needs to bring him to the stage when he is able to begin to read. No child should be held back, but the teacher's careful observation and her understanding of individual differences will help her to make sure that no one is forced into reading before he has

much chance of success. A few children may have begun to read when they come to school, but there will be others who require considerable additional experience and support. Some will need to gain confidence in themselves or to develop greater concentration, others will have little awareness of what reading means – young children often think they can read without really understanding the link between the printed and spoken word – and for others a much wider language background must be built up. The ordinary daily programme, with the adult's help, will provide the necessary basis of these skills for many children. For example when they are sorting and matching, comparing and making sequences, when they are playing 'I Spy' and listening to music or identifying the many background sounds around them, they are being helped to develop finer discrimination. In fact very many of the activities in the first school, coupled with an environment which draws attention to the printed word, are preparing the child for reading, although they may not be given the specific title of 'pre-reading' or 'reading readiness' programmes.

(c) Methods and approaches   Since children differ in so many ways, including the ways in which they learn, and since teachers have differing styles, it is not surprising that recent research does not indicate any one best method of teaching reading. The debate concerning methods has largely given way to a fuller consideration of the many factors involved in learning to read. In the early stages, children learn to recognise a number of words which are in their spoken vocabulary and which hold meaning for them, and this gives them interest and a feeling of success. Words about themselves and their daily lives are among the first to be acquired. At the same time, however, they are gradually acquiring understanding of the function of sounds and letters, often incidentally and through games. They notice that Margaret's name begins with the same letter as Michael's, and that there is a pattern of sound in 'sand' and 'band'. They will need a knowledge of the relationship between sounds and written symbols in order to decode words which they have not previously met in written form, and they will need also to learn to use the context of words to help in identifying them. As they become

more proficient they begin to take notice also of word and letter order, and use their knowledge of probable sequences to provide additional cues. The teacher draws from a variety of approaches, using elements from each at appropriate times, but reading with understanding is encouraged at all levels.

(d) Reading schemes Most schools make use of at least one published series of graded readers, which have the advantage of providing a controlled vocabulary and gradient of difficulty in sentence structure. Children are introduced to the characters in these books through pictures and stories, and usually when they are given their first book, most are so familiar with the words that they can read it straight through without hesitation. This gives great impetus to their efforts, and they are eager to take their books home to read to their parents. Unfortunately, in some cases, progress through graded readers is seen as the only worthwhile evidence of learning, whereas in fact it is only one part of the whole process. Reading should be reflected in the everyday life of the school, and is not a 'subject' set apart. Nevertheless, especially where groups are large and abilities and experience very varied, graded reading schemes play a valuable part in providing a planned sequence of learning.

A large number of reading schemes is now available, and the best of these have more appeal for children than some of the dull, repetitive series of the past. They are attractive in presentation, and their content is more interesting and relevant. The remoteness of the subject matter of some schemes from the real life of the children has been of concern to some researchers, who condemned the apparently self-satisfied 'semi-detached' existence often portrayed, and there have been various attempts to redress the balance. The Bullock Report asserts its conviction that 'children's experience should not be confined to a restricted range of reading matter presenting a narrow range of attitudes' (para. 7.17) and draws attention to aspects such as parental and sex roles and attitudes to authority, the presentation of which should be carefully considered. The need to relate the language patterns of the written text to children's experience of speech is also pointed out, and the 'stilted and unnatural' structures employed in some schemes are deplored because they prevent children from using their own knowledge of sentence structures in predicting what is likely to occur next in the sequence of words (para. 7.18). Teachers nowadays have a demanding task in making choices from the many alternatives, but many teachers' centres and reading centres have permanent exhibitions of reading schemes, and are also prepared to give guidance on selection.

Some children require a great deal of practice at all levels, and most will reach certain stages at which they seem to stick. They use materials, games and apparatus, either in connection with a reading scheme, or specially devised by the teacher, in order to consolidate skills, and their progress is carefully noted so that future work may be planned. Activities are informal, designed for individual or group use, but they are not haphazard. Many series of graded readers produce supplementary books at each level, and these give further practice. It is customary in many schools to introduce more than one reading scheme, in some cases after the initial stage, and opportunity is thus given for extensive reading at one level of difficulty. This method has the additional advantage of giving children experience of other styles of writing, and of broadening their interest, for early books are necessarily limited in vocabulary and involve much repetition. Careful progression is ensured by systems of grading, such as colour-coding, which enable both teacher and pupil to select books and materials quickly, choosing any book from the green series as reinforcement, for example, or moving on to the blue set.

Hearing children read is a major matter, and in addition to pursuing some reading activity daily, it is usually considered desirable that each child works with the teacher for a short period several times a week. From the child's point of view all that is desired is to be 'heard' from time to time, for he will be eager to share his achievement. If conversation about the subject matter follows he has had another valuable opportunity for connecting print and meaning. The teacher, however, does much more. She notes errors carefully so that she can check upon difficulties (for miscues have different origins, and she has to diagnose the kind of problem a child may have encountered).

(e) Some recent innovations   The difficulty which some children

have in learning to read has led to a great deal of research and experiment concerning the ways in which children are introduced to print. The consensus of opinion is that methods and schemes are of less importance than the skill of the teacher who uses them, the general approach and climate of the school and the overall development of the child. Nevertheless, any means whereby a child may be enabled to progress more pleasurably and efficiently is worthy of consideration, and teachers have been ready to try out new ideas, testing them critically and applying them where suitable to their own situation. One major stumbling-block in learning to read has always been the complexity of the English spelling system, and innovations have largely been concerned with ways of dealing with this. Some systems have used colour to help children to identify the pronunciation of symbols, either by letters having the same sound value in the same colour, as in *Words in Colour* (Gattegno 1969), or by giving particular sounds coloured backgrounds of different shapes as in *Colour Story Reading* (Jones 1967). The Bullock Committee's survey found a minority of schools using such systems, however, and still fewer who used a system of 'diacritical marking' – the marking of letters by symbols to indicate their sound value – but the report points out that 'although there is no substantial evidence to support the use of cueing techniques of one kind or another they are certainly not discredited by research. Whether or not to adopt them is a decision for the school' (para. 7.26).

More schools have adopted the modified spelling system devised by Pitman and known as the Initial Teaching Alphabet (i.t.a.), which received great publicity in its experimental stages in the early 1960s. Teachers who are dedicated to this system find that because children are freed from the restrictions of spelling complexities, they are able to express themselves more fluently in writing, without so much recourse to the teacher or reliance upon printed lists which can hold them back when they are using traditional orthography. As nearly as possible, one written symbol represents one sound only, and this consistency certainly reduces some of the early problems. A full evaluation of i.t.a. by Warburton and Southgate (1969) for the Schools Council, in which this point is made, gives an account of the evidence of both its advantages and drawbacks.

An approach which is a practical application of the principles of linguistics is *Breakthrough to Literacy* (Mackay, Thompson and Schaub 1970), produced as a result of the Schools Council Initial Literacy project. The authors believe that children's reading matter should be linked to their own spoken language as well as to their interests and experiences, and that the teacher should be 'an active participant in the child's learning process, constantly offering the child guidance and help'. *Breakthrough* is not a traditional reading scheme, and the materials introduced are intended to help the child to read and to produce written language from the beginning. The 'language-experience' approach which is used successfully by many teachers does this also, but children are often impeded by their lack of ability to write down or to spell the words they want to use. When they are progressing beyond the stage of dictating to the teacher and copying her writing, the volume of their output and its expressive quality can be restricted for these reasons. *Breakthrough* provides a basic selection of familiar words as printed cards, to which may be added a child's personal store, and which he then orders and organises into his own sentences in a holder. These are then read back, and copied by the teacher into his book as a personal reader. At a later stage he uses individual letter cards to make words. Many teachers who use this approach find that it gives great scope for original and inventive writing.

(f) Extending reading skills   After the initial stages more advanced children will be helped towards employing more complex skills. It is necessary to bear in mind the purposes for which we want them to read, so that provision is not neglected. We would hope that they will become people who read for pleasure, and who think about what they read, so that their personal development is fostered and their understanding and ability to analyse critically are developed. This involves access to a wide selection of literature and time to read it.

We would hope also that they would use reading to gain information, and so we would help them to learn, for example, how to use dictionaries and reference books, giving practice in such skills through

the pursuit of interests which arise from their experiences. Much
emphasis is placed upon this extension of reading skills beyond the
bare initial competence level, and if children are to remain in the first
school until they are eight or nine years old it is clearly essential that
their progress does not halt at this point. An interest in words can
also be developed at this stage, and children become absorbed in
seeking out alternative words similar in meaning, word derivations,
and words which echo the meaning they represent. This active interest is one of the most helpful allies for the teacher in encouraging
accurate spelling and lively language usage.

(g) Children's writing   When children's own language is accepted,
valued and extended, and when they have plenty of first-hand
experience which they want to communicate, there is usually little
problem in encouraging them to write. From the short statement
which accompanies early drawings, the children progress to writing,
often at great length. They will not always be asked to write about
their experiences, nor will they be instructed to 'write a story' each
day. They will write for different purposes – to give a factual account
or an explanation of how a model was made; to describe in detail a
particular building or animal they have seen; to express in their own
way, in prose or poetry, an experience which they have felt deeply, as
well as to invent a tale. Sometimes new impetus may be given by
writing something which is to be read by others for a specific purpose. A class in a rural school invited an urban 'neighbour' to spend a
day with them. This involved exchange of letters of invitation, acceptance and thanks, and in some cases a continued correspondence
which gave new meaning to those experiences which had to be put
into words to share with a friend.

Careful presentation of work is also encouraged by writing for a
purpose. These children appreciated that their letters must be legi-
ble, and the more advanced learned how to address the envelopes. A
whole range of interests, from mapping the postman's daily route to
finding out about the work of the Post Office, could be opened up,
which in turn would produce occasions for different sorts of writing.
When work is intended for special display, children are willing to
rewrite where necessary in order to present their best efforts, but as a

general rule emphasis should be placed first upon spontaneity and fluency in expression. Over-correcting can be extremely discouraging, and it tends to be the child who needs the most encouragement who collects the most corrections! This, however, is not to say that quality of presentation and good use of language are to be ignored. It is another instance of fitting our teaching to the occasion and to the individual child's requirements. It is therefore usual for a child to have some writing which is uncorrected and some in which a small number of regularly-used words are corrected. The teacher will take the opportunity to talk about problems to each child, or to a group or class where there are common errors which can be used as teaching points.

There will be a time when poor handwriting habits and hesitancy over spelling and punctuation decisions will inhibit the expression of children's ideas, and to fail to give help would defeat the original intention of promoting lively writing. Children are given frequent short practice periods in handwriting, and the teacher watches closely so that she can see when a child is using poor techniques which will lead to inefficiency. He may not know how to hold his pencil, or at which point to start forming a particular letter. She will then teach him individually or in a small group. Similarly, spelling and the general use of English are usually taught from words and passages of writing within the child's own experience rather than from published word-lists or formal exercises which may have little meaning for him, and which he may rarely apply to his own writing.

Listening, talking, reading, writing: if we stand back and reflect upon the aspects of human development which are affected by these, and if we consider too how the experiences we meet contribute to the way in which these skills are fostered, we become even more conscious of the responsibility which must be borne by the teacher of young children. The years from three to eight represent a large proportion of the early and critical learning period. Modern practice takes into account the fact that children must be allowed to develop at their own pace but at the same time deliberately organises teaching in appropriate situations. It allows for individual expression and informality, but admits the need for carefully planned sequences of learning and for practice of skills which do not 'just happen'. Furthermore, it encourages an integration of learning in which language skills feed into and are fed by all aspects of the curriculum.

7 Developing play experiences

Perhaps a remaining puritanical streak makes many people feel guilty about 'play' and consider it as an excuse for not doing what we ought to be doing – 'working'. It is an aspect of school experience which causes great confusion. Children go home daily and say, if parents enquire what they have done all day, 'just played' or 'nothing'. Recently an excellent infants teacher was told that now a particular child was in the junior school he was doing better because he was getting down to some work. We know the anxieties parents and teachers share when such statements are made. Perhaps the increased knowledge of the way in which children grow and develop will help disseminate greater understanding of the value of play.

The importance of play

Play can take so many forms: it can mean making mudpies, intensely exploring a material, messing about, having fun or seeming just to waste time. Children have a natural instinct for play and will develop it out of school and within school whether it is deliberately catered for or not. Children experience play at different levels of intensity; it varies from a solitary and extensive investigation of a material to a rumbustious chase round a classroom with Lego guns. It is the latter kind of play, a necessary social interaction within certain contexts, which brings the reputation of play in the school setting into question. There is little place for such disruptive repetitive play in a busy classroom and it is a misconception that this is encouraged in school. Despite the fact that children have greater freedom to move from one activity to another they are encouraged to enjoy their experiences within a framework which considers other people. A skilful teacher would re-direct the children to a more constructive activity.

Since the early days of nursery education teachers have recognised the importance of play. However it is only in recent years that its cognitive aspects have been increasingly understood. Flexible intelligence and learning are shaped by play. Without opportunities for play of every kind – solitary, with concrete objects, with animals, other children and most importantly with adults – a child will not develop fully reciprocal forms of communication. The nurture of emotional stability and the subsequent development of empathy will not be possible without sensitive responses to a child's communication through play.

Children do not need to be taught to be curious or to play. Although exposure to stress may damage this ability their natural desire to discover and explore their environments can be restored. It is only throught intense exploration that a fuller understanding of mathematical and scientific concepts can be achieved. Furthermore the child can come to appreciate adult roles and form his self-concept by role playing and through the social interactions of play. On passing the home corner Jane was heard pretending to be baby being sick. Then she switched to being mother. 'That's the third time you been sick today,' she said with an obvious mixture of sympathy and harassment at the thought of more washing and cleaning.

Although there are several categories of play (see Millar 1968) the most relevant to school experiences and provisions are exploring and practice play, and fantasy, feeling and make-believe play:

(a) Exploring and practice play   From the earliest days a child will engage in exploratory play and test out his effect upon the environment. He will work intensely with any new object to find out what impact he has upon the object and what it is capable of doing. After these explorations he will engage in what we generally call play. A baby of ten months was observed on a shingle beach sitting up beside his parents. He had two buckets, one of which was occasionally filled

with sea water. For about an hour he was totally engrossed in investigation of the shingle and water: dropping it from varying heights, running it through his fingers, patting it and pressing it. He was finding out a great deal about water and shingle. This is real learning of the most efficient kind. (Some psychologists believe that children learn more, and more efficiently, in the first five years than ever after.) This happens almost entirely through play. Piaget calls this period the sensori-motor stage. It characterises the first eighteen months of life. By the time children reach nursery school age they will have acquired a store of experiences of this type and will continue practising them as well as presenting additional challenges to themselves. For example two children in a department store might try jumping down from higher and higher steps on the stairs – a challenge tried by most children.

(b) Fantasy, feeling and make-believe play   As Susanne Millar states, make-believe play is at its height between the ages of about eighteen months and seven or eight years.

There is no one function of make-believe play. The child may be exploring his feelings, lessening his fears, increasing his excitement, trying to understand a puzzling event by graphic presentation, seeking confirmation of a hazy memory, or altering an event to make it pleasant to himself in fantasy. (Millar 1968)

Initially it takes the form of some simple repetition of a small actual event but gradually becomes more complex and elaborated, integrating real experiences with imaginary ones. Juxtaposing real events alongside invented ones characterises this kind of activity, as does elaborate language play. New words are invented and boxes, blankets and other objects symbolise all manner of things. Andrew, Philip and Jane – four- and five-year-olds playing pirates in the street – enjoyed talking about their role with an adult but when she enquired where they planned to sail to they looked at her somewhat pityingly and explained that their boat was not a real one. Children will switch readily from fact to fantasy and will usually be able to differentiate the two in their own play. When a new story is told to them they will check the accuracy of the information and ask 'Is it true?' or comment that it is only 'pretending'. In all these events they are classifying and reclassifying their experiences.

It is through make-believe play that children rehearse adult roles. They will put on a pair of adult shoes and be a lady. They can come to terms with some frightening events by imagining them as less painful, by distorting them or by constantly repeating them so that the impact becomes lessened. Miriam, whose mother was in hospital, constantly drew pictures of a little girl lost in the forest — an expression of her own subconscious feelings. The small child can be a giant crashing down on a building, the poor child a rich man dispensing wealth, a timid child a witch casting wicked spells over all her enemies. They will shriek in terror as they pretend a ladybird is some wicked monster. Thus fantasy can be a vehicle for emotional problem-solving and an anxiety-reducing activity. However it is also sheer exercise for the imagination to construct the amazing, ridiculous and absurd. Many of these interchanges are an overt communication between the child and himself. Gradually, as children develop, they will involve friends in their fantasy and compete with each other to relate the most outrageous tale or lay claim to some uncle who is bigger, 'cleverer' and more amazing than anyone else's. The teacher and her class will enjoy shared experiences both when she relates remarkable stories and when the children tell tall tales and make contributions to 'you'll never believe it' books or 'the strange present' or compile diets for witches, hobgoblins and dragons! As their store of experience and their ability to express themselves through reading and writing grow this type of play diminishes and is gradually replaced by group and gang play.

Pre-school experiences

Children will come to school having had a variety of experiences. Some live in high tower blocks where they have lacked play opportunities because of noise and safety problems, others may have roamed relatively freely in backstreets and mixed with older children, still others will have been restricted in their explorations by over-caring mothers and will have developed inhibitions and fears about getting dirty, while some children will have belonged to a good playgroup where there were plenty of social play opportunities. Some children will have extended the quality of their play through play with adults. Other children, either because they were members of large families or were looked after by inadequate child minders, will have had little interchange with adults. A child who has led a vigorous outdoor life may find school particularly strange. One wonders just what this farmer's son thought of school. At home, clad in wellingtons and muddy coat (an exact replica of his father) he was observed helping to herd the cows to the milking parlour. He trailed a huge stick behind him and urged the cows along using his father's language! How relevant would he find clay and paper work, or the home corner? At home he was concerned, not with the long-term aims of becoming 'educated' or a 'good citizen,' but with the practicalities of getting the cows milked and bedded down for the night. What did he think of the female-dominated world of school? Perhaps not very much! Another child may be expecting school to be analogous to one long delightful party — his parents may have stressed the exciting aspects of school to such an extent that he finds taking turns and having to wait for an adult's attention particularly frustrating. He may perhaps have been dressed up in his 'best' clothes to come to school, which he has been exhorted to keep clean. (A teacher ought to insist that children roll up their sleeves and wear protective clothing for designated activities — but not *all* teachers take this kind of care and many a parent is presented with a powdered, painted, glued and messy child at home-time.) A child who comes from a home where being a 'good boy' has been constantly stressed, may be uncertain how to respond to playing with materials like clay. At home he thinks of this as 'mud' and therefore something to be avoided if he does not wish to incur his mother's wrath! It is amazing that so many children do, in fact, learn to cope so well with the strangely contradictory world we present to them.

The sensitive teacher will recognise that her provision should meet a variety of needs. For example the child who has had many outdoor play opportunities with older children will need the experience of quieter more contained play where finer motor skills can be developed and will certainly need the stimulus of adult conversation. Others may find large classes and school activities altogether far too stimulating and we may need to rethink our provision for these children.

The teacher's part

The main roots of the growth of the mind are the development of play and of language. The teacher's part will be to foster rich experiences within these areas. How can she best achieve this? Rich provision will not suffice alone. It must be adjusted to need. Perhaps the analogy of a dietician will be helpful. A good dietician provides a rich and varied diet, which would include the staples of life. However, occasionally she would introduce a new food or lessen the richness of the diet in order to prevent over-stimulation. She would have to provide special diets for some and occasionally, in consideration of particular problems, everyone's diet may have to be adjusted to accommodate individual stresses. For example, when Mother's Day came around one teacher suggested her class made cards for grandmothers, aunts, big sisters, fathers or any person who helped them, for Wendy's mother had died and Michael's mother had left home without letting her family know where she was. Most importantly the teacher needs to interact with the children. How is this possible with thirty or more children? It is amazing to see how effectively a teacher can interact in different ways with groups and individuals almost simultaneously. She will make judgements about when to intervene to extend an idea and when to stand back to let a child solve problems. Naturally she cannot always be right. Clearly there will be occasions when she misses the opportune moment to intervene or when she curtails the development of play by her questions. Nevertheless, her enthusiasm for poking, wondering, prying and finding out will act as a great motivator. The greater opportunity for child interaction also means that often thirty-one people are supporting each other rather than there being one teacher trying to cope with thirty children.

The good teacher can build upon the child's direct experiences by asking meaningful questions. She is unlikely to supply immediate answers except in such matters as helping a child spell a word correctly, for she will take a long-term view of education and will rather help a child to refine and enrich his experiences. As the Chinese saying goes, 'Give a man a fish and you feed him for a day. Teach him how to fish and you feed him for life'.

All this must sound daunting to many readers! It certainly calls for teachers of a high calibre. However teachers are not 'born'. Usually they have three or four years' initial professional education and numerous opportunities to go on developing expertise. Demands upon them are greater than ever but there has been a parallel although lesser growth in support for the teacher. Some education authorities appoint special advisory teachers whose main responsibility is to support and encourage young teachers. These advisors arrange meetings and visits with other probationers (teachers in their first year of teaching) so that problems and successes can be shared. We can go on developing, growing, learning from successes and mistakes, from interchanges with colleagues and parents and continually deepen our understanding of children and our abilities to motivate them.

The support for newly qualified teachers is therefore variable. The pressures upon them at the start of their careers are often enormous – and this may be combined with living alone or running a household for the first time. In school they may be exhorted to give the rest of the staff plenty of 'new' ideas, but be virtually left to 'sink or swim' in the classroom. They worry about how they will relate to parents and wonder if parents will find their youth and inexperience acceptable. They will need not only encouragement but practical help – which is not always forthcoming.

There can be serious problems of alienation or conflict for those teachers whose ideas differ sharply from the dominant ethos of the school. Many people would advocate such a teacher moving to a school more compatible with her working style and educational ideas. But how realistic a suggestion is this? Many teachers in first schools are married women, often with families, who chose to work at the nearest school to their home, and will not be anxious to add to their journeys. This kind of conflict of views can lead to disruption in a school, although teachers using very different teaching strategies sometimes work alongside each other quite happily. This seems less likely to happen in the nursery or open plan school. Compatible teachers, however, may see their differences as complementary.

It helps to work alongside colleagues with common aims, objectives and vision and to have a head teacher who sees that 'this vision, corporately determined, is corporately understood and implemented' (Pluckrose 1975).

Of course all the days will not run smoothly. There will be frustration and pitfalls, days seemingly full of accidents, spilled milk and paint, times when we feel despondent about William's standstill growth, Peter's continued aggressiveness, Baljit's lack of English and Sonya's poor physical condition. But thankfully all this will be counterbalanced with days when William shows real interest, Peter behaves kindly towards a distressed child and when everyone seems to take a positive step forward.

Provision for play experiences

Developments in early childhood education have reflected the growing appreciation of the influence play has upon a child's understanding. A typical classroom provides a variety of contexts for play of a therapeutic and educational type. Some of these points are illustrated in the following case study.

The home corner: case study We will not dwell upon the examples of apologies for 'homes' that lurk in corners of some classrooms. We are considering here a home corner that is well equipped with cookers, pots, pans, food packets, chairs, table, curtains, baby dolls, etc. Here a child can rehearse adult roles or replicate some home experience in order to come to terms with it. He can re-explore a frightening or worrying experience or express the jealousy he feels for the new baby by being angry and aggressive with the inanimate baby, be a baby again or a mother or father or a wayward child. He will learn greater control and a closer understanding of others and their viewpoints by this rehearsal, replication and regression. Not all the performances will be tragedies for he will repeat and perhaps share amusing and happy events, re-savouring them with relish. These opportunities for learning to cope with emotions can be as important as the extension of language and mathematical skills. However the provision in this corner of current radio and television papers, shopping lists, telephones and note pads, recipes, writing pads, stamps and envelopes, and real empty packets of a variety of household goods facilitates good play and helps develop reading and writing skills in relevant contexts. The children are encouraged to plan ahead, to think what they might need for their tea party or supper, and to record it (or if they are unable to write the teacher does it for them). The sorting and positioning of objects, setting of tables, placing of cups on hooks and plates in piles, the ironing and folding of clothes, the dressing of dolls in correctly sized clothes, and the re-decoration of the house (which involves the children in making, measuring and hanging wallpaper and new curtains), these and many other things are all valuable mathematical experiences.

Sometimes, either at the child's initiation or a teacher's, the home corner is changed into some other social setting. In this class the knowledge that in a few weeks' time the school doctor was coming to examine all the reception class children led the home to be changed into a surgery. All the paraphernalia of a surgery was assembled, the white-coated doctor examined his patients with care, recorded the ailments and prescribed treatments. The rather long queues during surgery hours (with old magazines to read to keep up the authenticity) reflected widespread hypochondria. Prescriptions were written out and taken to the chemist's shop of a nearby class and the symbols on the eye chart supported current phonic work. Not only were the children prepared for the doctor's visit but also many important aspects of the curriculum were catered for incidentally. The real school doctor visited the surgery, was delighted with the idea and talked briefly to the children. To confirm one part of the value of much of this play not one child in the class cried when they visited the doctor and received an injection.

Perhaps the home corner development illustrates how the teacher is deliberately extending the children's abilities in every possible direction.

Physical activities

There will be many informal opportunities for extending and practising physical skills, particularly in the nursery school. Spatial skills
develop as a child constructs with building blocks or avoids colliding
with another child's work. Finer motor skills grow as they use
scissors, hold paintbrushes, fasten buttons, make large jigsaws and
handle all types of materials. Mathematical concepts are developed
as children discover 'weightiness' by lifting solid blocks or boxes of
sand. The relationship of weight to capacity and the difference
between solid and liquid become meaningful through their physical
manipulation of sand and water.

The school may provide a variety of apparatus such as climbing
frames, ropes and slides and may have retained hillocks and other
contours of land outside on the site. Those children who have been
confined for social or safety reasons may need extended opportunities to develop their gross motor skills and the flexibility of the
timetable will present such opportunities. When he first started
school Nigel, aged five, who lived in a tiny one-roomed flat, rushed
around wildly. His teacher gave him plenty of opportunities to play
outside and often he accompanied the school caretaker around the
grounds. Gradually he settled down to the overall rhythm of the
school.

As children grow older they will extend their physical prowess in
physical education lessons. This is one of the aspects of the
curriculum which may require timetabling as the hall space often has
to be shared by others. Many children relish the increasing control
they gain over their bodies and set themselves targets such as
reaching a higher point on the climbing ropes. Children will be encouraged to develop their own skills and will not be expected all to
achieve the same standards. The aim would be for each child to im-
prove upon his own best performance rather than to compete with
his neighbour.

One problem which still remains in some schools is playtime.
Many schools have dropped playtimes as these frequently in-
terrupted the rhythm of the day and took up a disproportionate

amount of time for their worth. As children are no longer confined to their desks for long periods, 'letting off steam' is unnecessary. Some schools adopt some of the flexibility of nursery schools and have out-door experiences available for a few children throughout most of the day, or, if space allows, some indoor physical play opportunities. However the problem of the hour-long play period after lunch remains with us and perhaps one might consider shortening the time.

One example of the inter-relatedness of all aspects of development might be worth noting. One of the most relevant mathematical experiences for one group of children occurred during a physical education period. Mark, Emma and Peter who were using ropes suddenly became involved in noticing the floor area their ropes covered. Soon the whole class was coiling, twisting and reshaping ropes to find out who could cover the least or most area with ropes of the same length. To the incredulity of other staff members the class decided that, for maximum area enclosed per unit of hedge, fields ought to be round!

Mathematical play

To understand the rationality and relevance of computation a child will need many opportunities, both structured and incidental, to measure, weigh, construct, count, divide and estimate. The classroom will contain many facilities for these extensions of play. A teacher may place small red and blue plastic toys together knowing that this is likely to cause a child to classify them according to colour. The use of bricks, sand, water and other constructional materials will facilitate the development of such processes as comparison and reversibility. For example he will compare the levels of water in two identical jars, and agree that they are the same, but he will need a lot of experience in handling water before he will be able to see that if the contents of one jar are poured into two smaller jars these two will still contain the same amount of water as the original one. The children will not usually be taught facts in isolation from their experiences. Instructing a child about water displacement is not so effective as stepping in with further related problems when a child fills a bath to the top and then puts the baby in during home corner play. Ready access to materials can help to initiate and support the child's ability to question, probe, make judgements, test out hypotheses and cope with and adjust to problems. Nevertheless, it is the strategies a teacher adopts to extend and unfold a child's thinking which remain crucial.

Although great emphasis has been placed upon the need to provide a secure base for the children's work this does not exclude children from facing problems, challenges, and difficulties both with materials and in co-operation with others. Were they protected from all this it would produce an entirely distorted picture of the real world. Many of the conflicts which arise between young children are concerned with sharing toys or with one child destroying another's work, when the children involved may well resort to fighting. Clearly long homilies on these occasions will be useless, but we have found it effective, with first school children, to contrast human with animal problems in communication. Animals may have to resort to biting and scratching but human beings have the gift of language and can say 'I'm sorry' and 'You can have a turn next'. Clearly it is very frustrating for a child when his work is destroyed by others. His natural instinct will be to hurt the aggressor in some way and both the attacked and attacker will need help in coming to terms with their behaviour. A teacher will have to make her class understand other children's work must not be interfered with.

The good teacher tries to encourage a child to seek solutions to his mathematical problems but, because she knows her children well, does not push them to the limits of frustration or towards meeting constant failure. She helps the child find the most suitable materials to use for his space-ship, gets him to estimate the amount of cloth he needs to make a batman cape, encourages him to make imaginative selections of textures for a collage and generally helps him to verbalise his thoughts and feelings so that he can be led towards greater understanding and success.

Because many adults, including some teachers, have become virtual prisoners of the narrowness of their own mathematical experiences, we do not always see the mathematical and scientific connections being made in many activities. Some people have developed fears and inhibitions about mathematics – comparing it to a necessary, but nasty, dose of medicine. Rather than actual calculation of the school hall floor area, we as children were involved in problems about hypothetical baths filling and emptying, often at peculiar rates. But the children of today will be seeing what they can do in a minute – how many strides they can take, whether they can complete a simple jigsaw or fill the kettle. They will be cooking and baking, which involves a number of mathematical processes. They will discover facts about area and volume in their constructional work and when clearing and tidying up, packing articles into their appropriate boxes. They have far greater autonomy and responsibility than we had as children – quite young children may be put in charge of the class or school 'crisps' shop. They will count the daily takings and perhaps accompany the school secretary to deposit the money in the bank.

Class and school shops have already been mentioned in other connections, but perhaps the mathematical links are the most obvious. Think of the opportunities for counting money, sorting stamps, writing letters, cashing postal orders, 'purchasing' birthday and Christmas cards and sending them through the internal delivery service. The really imaginative teacher will see possibilities in all manner of situations, and will ensure that the child makes a record of some of his mathematical discoveries. This may be done pictorially or in copied written symbols in a class or individual book.

Structural mathematical apparatus and schemes

Several interesting advances have taken place in the development of structural materials designed to help foster mathematical understanding. Apparatus such as Dienes Blocks, Cuisenaire rods and Unifix cubes present many opportunities for children and adults to see mathematical principles and processes in terms of concrete action. Children are likely to have a better concept of what ninety-eight means if they can make this number along a hundred track by placing blocks of ten units and single units inside the track. Then they may not go home as Helen did and say she was learning how to do 't's and u's' without having any real understanding that this meant tens and units or what quantity the numbers stood for. Usually this type of structural apparatus would form one segment of the 'mathematical cake' provided for children.

Fletcher's mathematical books (1970) have been available for some time in this country. These provide a teacher's manual and workbooks for children to use to develop their numeracy. Many teachers find the teacher's manual a fruitful source of ideas for developing work cards for their classes. Others let the children use the workbooks as their sole mathematical experience. This seems most unfortunate since, like the structured apparatus, such things ought to provide just another segment of experience.

However, it is useful to have some guideline to check whether or not children have really understood the meaning of numbers – that seven is not only seven but two more than five and three less than ten and so on. So another scheme called *Beginning Mathematics* provides useful ways of checking understanding as well as presenting interesting ideas for the development of work cards (Sealey and Gibbon 1965).

Scientific experiences

Most situations will be exploited for their scientific potential. The routine dental checks will be an ideal time to count, draw and paint teeth and help eradicate any irrational fears of the dentist, short simple truthful explanations being usually the best policy. The care of class animals provides not only an opportunity for demonstrating and sharing responsibility for their welfare but gives early instruction about feet, beaks, skin and the birth and tending of young. The child who needs extra comfort or opportunities to show affection can often do this more effectively by his contacts with animals who make less overt demands than many adults. Much of the early scientific explorations will have strong biological and environmental connections. Full use can be made of free commodities like the weather! The following incident took place on a beautiful sunny frosty morning.

The ice experiments: case study A few children from different classes in the school were gathered together along the banks of the brook which ran through the school grounds. The night temperature had been very low and so the brook was frozen. The ice near the house-boat and beneath the willow trees was thinner. Why was this, they wondered? Martin managed to lift a section of the ice. A teacher from another class joined them and seized on their interest to develop the situation. Instead of merely supplying the children with answers she posed further questions which would in turn answer the children's initial question. Could they preserve the ice in any way? If pieces of ice of the same dimensions were put in different places what would happen? What would be the quickest and most effective way of melting the ice? Would the texture of the area where the ice was placed have any effect on the way it melted? The children set about these and many more problems. They timed and recorded their experiments and thoroughly enjoyed working together from this incidental grouping and beginning.

The more recent developments in the classroom have been a recognition of the worth of many of these 'play' experiences and the major possibilities they present for the consolidation and extension of the children's abilities. They represent the increasing emphasis and move towards developing children's cognitive abilities through interaction with their environment.

8 Using the environment

In the past we tended in teaching to ignore the riches on our doorstep, for familiarity often blunts the sharpness of our perceptions. We used to concentrate on far-off environments, touching on such subjects as rubber tapping in Malaysia. It is not that these things are entirely irrelevant, for television has made these environments more familiar. However the use of our own localities has the great advantage of not only being cheap and readily accessible but rooted in the familiar and concrete. Thus it helps to make a child feel confident and comfortable. We can readily return to them to clarify information. We can look at the beech wood at different seasons and watch the growth of a motorway or housing development.

Bringing in the outside world

Perhaps, without perceiving it in an environmental way, the nursery and infant schools have traditionally brought more of the 'outside' world into their classrooms than junior and secondary schools. Provisions for domestic play have brought the home literally into a corner of the classroom. The classroom shop, at the nursery level mainly another opportunity for social play, was an attempt to weld the infant school child's experiences out of school with a practical way of developing mathematical skills. Young children are interested in natural objects and so most classrooms would include a nature table. They are such an accepted part of the classroom that they can be rather dusty accumulations of wizened conkers and decaying heaps of vegetation, present but undiscussed, and rarely glanced at, but at best they are immensely interesting collections, beautifully displayed and cared for, yet constantly added to by teachers, parents and children.

As the curriculum widened so did the concept of what was considered appropriate material for classroom usage. More and more man-made materials such as boxes, cogs, packaging and plastic tubing were used either in art and craft activities or as objects to be investigated on discovery tables.

Re-exploring the immediate surroundings

We began to take greater cognisance of the experiences children brought to school with them and used them more to invite children to re-explore their surroundings. Children, with the freshness of their senses, often perceive the minutiae around them more alertly than adults. This can be considerably reinforced if teachers are seen to share their sensitivity and enthusiasm. We have moved a long way from the idea that in order for an outing to be worthwhile it needed to be an expensive trip to a zoo, the perhaps distant seaside, or a main post office. It does not matter how rudimentary the objective of an exploratory exercise is. One nursery teacher simply took small groups of children for a short drive in her car down a particularly beautiful avenue of autumn trees with shafts of October sunlight shining through them. The sheer joy of a shared experience helps to reinforce positive and happy relationships between teacher and child. It is then possible to share again these reassuring moments when we have 'do you remember when' sessions.

It is generally only in the nursery school situation, because of the better teacher–child ratio, that frequent spontaneous outings with small groups of children are possible. The safety of children is a major responsibility and with the three- to five-year-olds one would expect one adult to accompany five children, with one adult for each group of ten children above that age. The degree of flexibility for 'unplanned' visits in the first school will depend upon the availability of ancillary and voluntary help. Most visits are carefully planned in advance so that relevant books and materials can be collected, but if the road is being dug up or trees being felled near the school no good teacher is going to miss this interesting opportunity to let the children observe the work.

We have tried to emphasise the wide developmental period covered by the three- to eight-year-old age range; so that although the use of the environment will have many common aspects and objectives these will tend to become more diversified and specific as children mature. In most respects it matters less what the content of the visit is than that the experience adds positively in some way to a child's developmental needs and helps him to question, probe and discover more with the support of the informational resources in the school. The expectations of the work which will arise from any visit need to be realistic but it is remarkable what can evolve if the teacher takes time and trouble to reinforce and support the visit with the use of various resources. In our fast moving society, however, sometimes it is enough just to look at the autumn trees. Although we make many demands upon children to use these concrete experiences one hopes that every event will not have to be written, drawn, painted, danced, sung, measured and calculated!

Planning for progression

The use of the environment ought to form a vital part of the curriculum, although young children especially may concentrate on different aspects of the visit and often notice things beyond the teacher's intention! The teacher who took a downtown class to the airport found the highlight of the event was the free orange squash they were served at a newly opened motorway café which they visited quite by chance. Likewise, another teacher taking her class on a similar visit found that the escalator and the stone chippings surrounding the plant troughs in the lounge areas provided the major interest.

Some children are never or hardly ever taken out in a family group and so they are able to benefit particularly from this type of shared experience. Of the practical examples which follow, some arose incidentally and others were more detailed and elaborated attempts to extend children's knowledge and skills. Many of the examples would be appropriate experiences for any first school child. However, as we move up the age range under consideration children might have similar experiences but the level of demand for abstraction and analysis of the information would be more extensive. We must beware of what has been named 'trundlewheelitis' (a trundlewheel is a stick with a wheel attached for measuring distances in yards or metres). We must be certain that children are not repeating similar experiences without extra demands being made upon them. They might trundlewheel the perimeter of their playground at six, seven, eight and far into the secondary school. This is acceptable, if the secondary school children are making increased use of the collected data as a surveyor would, but fruitless otherwise. This does not apply to everything; we can go on exploring such things as paint indefinitely. It is vital that the teachers of older children make themselves familiar with the kinds of experiences that have already been presented to children in their first schools; it could be a revelation to many.

The listening walk: case study   Have you ever stopped to consider just how many different sounds you hear even in a short space of time? Although this kind of experience is not necessarily at the level of fine auditory discrimination it is a valuable and revealing experiment. It is by no means a new idea but teachers need to remember to repeat such interesting experiences to different generations of children.

The school in this example was in the middle of a slum clearance rehousing development. The houses, although relatively new, were drab and what few trees had been planted were either damaged or struggling to survive. At first glance the outlook for any interesting environmental work seemed bleak. We took the children out of school to 'listen' for ten minutes only. Remarkably, we heard thirty-five sounds. Glynn heard the soft whirl of a bicycle wheel, Nicola the thud of a car door being slammed and Christopher noticed the crackle of a garden fire. We came back, recorded the experiences and made them into a class book. The class was vertically grouped and those who could write on their own did so while others drew and dictated to me what they wished to say, and then copied it. Everyone was expected to make a contribution and did this cheerfully. Everyone was also expected to make a special effort for this class book because we would use it for reference to re-explore our experience. The initial listening theme was developed over a period of weeks as a small but integral part of the day. We did not discuss the work every day but returned when it seemed appropriate, or when a child or group initiated more discussion. We talked about, and recorded in a book, the sounds we liked and did not like. Everyone had plenty of ideas about the latter. It makes one remember just how sensitive young children are to noise. This ought to cause teachers seriously to question some of their organisational methods and to ensure that exciting and interesting experiences are interspersed with plenty of calmness and tranquillity. We listened to records of bird songs and train sounds. We collected and laughed about many nonsense sounds the children had made up on their own or we devised together, as well as many collections of bangs, scrapes, crashes, hums and pings. An extension into our singing, movement and dance was a natural development. We improvised our own sounds by tapping objects, humming and chanting. A group of boys became interested in musical instruments and we hunted around for pictures and information. We all seemed to have sharpened our listening perception.

This manner of approaching work ensures that everyone has a chance of making a contribution. Those children who can sing beautifully or dance or listen with fine discrimination, even if their reading and writing skills are limited, have an opportunity to receive positive reinforcement. One hastens to add that a teacher ought to try to do as much as possible to develop a child's skills, but children will tend to acquire them by very different routes – devious in some cases and entirely straightforward in others. Susan's parents congratulated her teacher for the wonderful way she had taught Susan to read, but this five-year-old was one of those fortunate children who read without any difficulty. With Roger it was a very different story — a slow process not helped by his mother becoming more and more anxious about his progress. Eventually she was persuaded to let him join the library and select his own stories for her to read to him (she had not thought it worth doing this until he could read) and before he left the infant school he began to take some more hesitant steps in the direction of reading. Certainly Roger was one of the people who would have benefited by an additional year in the infant school.

Using current events

The sharp line of demarcation between home and school experience continues to fade. It is considered appropriate to use all manner of local, national and international events as sources of inspiration.

Traditional and seasonal events are used to help extend many skills. State weddings and funerals and such things as Prince Charles' 'investigation' as one six-year-old put it, are useful for there will also be opportunities at home to see something of these events. Scrap books, school newpapers and magazines can be put together right across this age range.

When Christmas comes it can appear that school has become nearly as commercial as the High Street. One could be quite critical of the amount of time spent on some activities — children practising carols until they are tired of them, and teachers becoming more and more harassed until the original idea of a joyous shared experience diminishes. The competition between teachers to produce the best decorations and Christmas concert can often result in the events being totally teacher-dominated or even in teachers producing the art work. This presents a wrong impression of what children can produce and parents may be confused when their child does 'infant' drawings at home and adult-like collage at school. Yet at its best Christmas time in school can be an especially happy time for reinforcing school and community bonds.

It is important that the woman teacher arms herself with information about the major football teams and the present popular heroes, either real or from some television serial. She will need to consider the interests of both boys and girls and make certain that her knowledge and provisions for boys' interests are extensive, for there is a quite serious lack of contact with men teachers in the early childhood education years. A number of women teachers feel inadequate about mathematics and science, and there is a possibility here of the first school continuing a cycle of deprivation. Teachers should also be aware of sex differences in learning: girls usually develop language abilities before boys, and there is a danger that teachers may concentrate upon formalising these skills to the detriment of the acquisition of spatial skills. Conversely boys, generally much better at spatial skills, receive even greater reinforcement by having extended opportunities to use constructional materials. Indeed in some classrooms block building is considered solely a boys' activity.

Extending children's interests

As children develop they may well become involved in some long-term environmental projects. They become increasingly aware of the environment through studying pollution in their area or the ecology of a piece of woodland. As nature trails develop no doubt more schools will use them and even help develop them. A nature trail is a planned route through various types of countryside giving detailed information of vegetation, trees, animals and birds inhabiting the area. Several local educational authorities have made excellent use of former school buildings by turning them into Field Centres of various kinds. Children from urban and rural environments can benefit from visits to these centres. One centre is in a former village school adjacent to the banks of a canal. The Warden is particularly knowledgeable about the canal banks and the water life, so children find it fascinating to explore this environment with him. They then have the opportunity of drawing the canal and its inhabitants, perhaps examining specimens through a microscope and recording and classifying their findings. If such centres are not near at hand teachers can use other schools in contrasting environments, for country children have much to gain from a visit to a city environment.

One of the frustrations of being seven or eight years old, especially if you are a younger member of a family, is that there seems an endless number of things that you are not old enough to do yet – the cry 'Wait until you are older' occurs incessantly. Although one cannot and would not want to hasten the kind of maturity parents refer to when they speak in this way, schools can sometimes give children a chance to experience independence and adventure early. One school provided a really exciting opportunity for the seven-year-olds in their final term before they left the infant school. This was an expedition for two nights to a field centre about eight miles from the school. The idea of going camping (although not under canvas) was especially appealing. The confidence and status the children gained in two and half days was quite remarkable. Karen who was the youngest member of a family of much older children clearly benefited. They worked and played hard, completed a study of plant life and the village, had a sing song around a camp fire and responded really well. Some parents visited their children in the evenings. All the children knew it would be possible to return home swiftly if necessary, but no one wanted to! The idea of infants camping may appear revolutionary and indeed many practicalities would have to be considered. One would have to see that children were not excluded because their parents were unable to afford the small contribution for the stay and that there were not problems about night clothes and other facilities, but in this instance there were no such difficulties.

Such events as the one above are of course still quite rare and will probably continue to take place only on one or two occasions in the school year. But the garage, the supermarket, the farm, field or factory may be on our doorstep. People in the community are usually especially kind to younger children and give freely and unstintingly of their time. One old lady visited her local school to talk to groups of children about her Victorian childhood. She dressed up in a period nightgown and cap and fascinated the children with the details of her early experiences. This type of approach using remembered history seems a most applicable introduction to the study of other times for the upper age ranges of the first school.

The individual and his environment

One of the sharpest contrasts between work of the past and present, in the first school, is the greater opportunity for the child to demonstrate his own experience gathered during out-of-school sessions. The chances to draw, paint, write and talk about personal experiences are abundant. Paul, a five-year-old whose father kept pigs, was able to share his knowledge of sows, piglets, cleaning out and feeding routine and also the hilarity of the occasion when the largest sow was persuaded into his father's van. It is impossible for a child to be missed out, for all children have experiences they can talk about. That of James, noticing the rainbow patterns left by petrol on the road, can be seen as different from that of Lisa recounting a flight back to see grandma in the West Indies but it is as valid as an experience. It may take a teacher a little longer to unlock some child's capacity to recall and relate experiences if he has been inhibited or neglected or is shy or immature. His previous conditioning and expectation of what is appropriate for discussion in school means he may already consider his ideas 'unsuitable', for his concept of school may have been gained from the rather harsh 'playing at school' rituals performed by other children. Schools make the fullest use of children's work by collating it in class books about mothers, fathers, brothers, sisters, their dens and secret places, their dogs and cats, their favourite games, television programmes, and their thoughts, feelings, likes and dislikes concerning many things. The teacher too, is much more inclined to share her personal experiences with her class. She is much more likely to write some interesting additional information, question or comment upon the children's written work than the old tick. Timothy aged six typed this story:

One day there was a boy and he lived in a flat in London and his unkull lived in America and one day he was going to his uncle this week he was going to his uncle so he hat to get a few early nights then he wodnt be tirded on his jrnee to America it will be a very long jrnee it took him 99 days to get there and 99 days to get back as soon as he got home he went strat to bed with a hot cup of coaco and a plate full of sausages on sticks.

The teacher wrote:

My goodness he must have been exhausted travelling for all those days. He is lucky to eat sausages on sticks in bed, it sounds a special treat. I did enjoy this story Timothy.

Thus she constantly helps the child construct positive pictures of himself and his experiences. The comments are so varied the child eagerly clamours to know what it says; this approach is a great motivator.

The building site: case study   It was the beginning of the second half of the autumn term in school. Picture a class of enthusiastic eight-year-old boys and girls in a school encouraging an integrated approach to topic work and use of the environment, with a building site within two minutes walk of the school. It was too good an opportunity to miss. Having gained permission for the children to visit the site, a scheme of work was prepared using the heading of 'Our Building Project'.

Firstly, a flow diagram was designed to show possible areas of development mainly for the teacher's use (see figure 8.1, p. 105). This flexible approach allowed for the interests of the children to be followed both individually and collectively. Secondly, a library of books was added to the book corner as a reference point for both teacher and children.

In order to cover as much ground as possible, and to add to the classroom environment as fully as possible, the children were asked to work in four mixed ability groups. Unexpectedly, they decided to elect four group leaders who then selected their group members. This was a new experiment in social interaction and co-operation for the children. Next, the children were each given a folder and paper. A discussion was held as to what our project would or could be concerned with.

To introduce activities using the immediate and familiar environment the children were asked to remember their individual routes to school, and to look at their own homes in terms of construction and layout. The following day they looked at different types of houses with emphasis on representing layout and introducing the concept of mapping. Each group looked at something different and covered

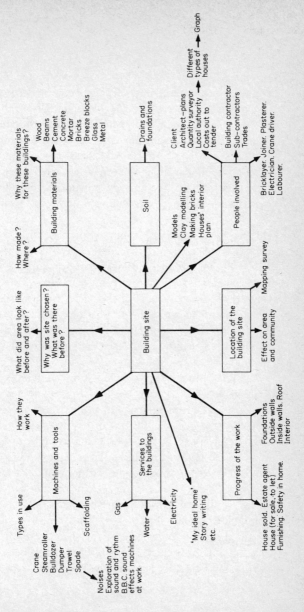

Figure 8.1 Integrated theme – the building site

mapping of school routes, the classroom and written and illustrated work on various types of housing. They started their classroom display by exhibiting examples of mapping. Techniques were discussed and conclusions reached as to the best way of mapping a route or representing the classroom. This background work was to make the building site, with its houses at different stages of construction, more meaningful. Now it was necessary to look at materials which would help the children discover information on their visit to the site. They looked at building materials, machine tools, the progress of buildings and services. These investigations were backed with visual materials such as pamphlets obtained from the gas, electricity and water boards and posters from manufacturing companies. A film strip was shown which described the various stages in the construction of a house.

Following these preliminary activities, work cards with a number of questions were given to the group leaders. They in turn discussed the questions with their group and allocated each child a question to find the answer to during the visit to the site. It took some time to get the children to settle down and look at the questions. Some children requested that others who were being troublesome be made to sit and stop making a fuss. Some said that they could not get anyone to listen! However after teething troubles some kind of order was established within the individual groups. As we said before, the children were not used to this type of activity. As might be expected, some of the less able were unsure of their ground and needed a great deal of attention and encouragement to enable them to continue within their discussion groups. Others withdrew because of their uncertainties. Some problems were resolved: for example, the groups asked if children such as Christopher, a quiet withdrawn poor reader, and Stephen, a boisterous quarrelsome virtual non reader, might 'draw a picture' to illustrate the answer to some task set for them by their group leaders. This was readily agreed to and the children complimented on finding a solution to the problem.

Having ensured that wellingtons or strong shoes were worn, and stressed the safety aspects of the visit, the teacher and class set out on their visit to the building site. Fortunately, the workmen were not busy and were able to talk to the children. Also the gas, electricity and water boards had vans on the site and the representatives were most helpful. The children were seen by their group leaders and an attempt was made to pace out the main through road for mapping purposes later. Objects were collected to take to the classroom for investigation.

On returning to the classroom the children wrote about what they had seen and discovered by talking to the workmen and by their own observation. It was at this point that many spontaneous activities took place. Avenues for investigation were pinpointed and selected, the original flow chart being borne in mind. Although the children were seated in their groups, they still preferred to work individually or with a 'friend'. It was interesting to see Christopher, an individual usually on the outside of group activities, take an old battery found on the site and attempt to discover its properties. He wanted to known how a battery works and was given a working battery and bulb to experiment with. As Christopher usually ended up by writing about battleships, whatever the current point of interest within the classroom, this activity of his was welcomed. Stephen took an opposite turn and refused to take part in any activity connected with the project. As usual he had to be reprimanded and confined to his desk. It was hoped that something would spark off his interest as the project continued. Some other boys found bricks most interesting and asked if they could investigate their properties. It was suggested that they leave them in water after weighing them, to test for absorbtion qualities. Three other boys took a quantity of squared paper and completed the map of the through road. They represented each pace with one square. On finding that five pieces of graph paper were needed we discussed the question of scale.

On assessing the work done so far, it seemed that Stephen was the only class member not yet involved although he was still included in discussion groups and class points of interest.

Having completed various tasks, and pursued interesting aspects of the topic, we looked at the planning of a house, from architect to buyer. Plans were provided for investigation. The class looked at foundations, discussing what they were for and experimented with a ruler pressed into damp sand. Damp courses were looked at with an experiment using sugar cubes, ink and foil. The children all had a turn with the experiments and some chose to write down the results – for example, that the flat of the ruler would not press into the sand as easily as the side; therefore a large flat area is needed to take the weight of a house. With the cubes, the ink rose only to the level of the foil, which represented a damp course.

It was really from these initial investigations of points of interest that the project became the children's. Now there was a lot of individual work being carried out. It was felt that the working in groups should not be compulsory but left up to the children.

The children looking at bricks were supplied with bricks at various stages of manufacture, and literature was displayed showing how bricks are made. They branched into doing brick rubbings, and finding interesting patterns within the school bricks, this in turn leading to making rubbings of various articles with different textures. Other children became interested in the construction of houses, in particular the fitting of a roof. They looked at the shape of a roof and asked why it was usually triangular. The children made shapes with triangles and tried to find out, with shapes made from strips of card and pins, which shapes are the strongest. Scaffolding was looked at, which led to the use of rolled newspaper for making both two- and three-dimensional objects. The girls in particular were interested in constructing three-dimensional models showing the interior of a house. They became very expert in making tiny pieces of furniture. This led to thinking about furnishing a home and the costs involved. The boys in the class also came around to constructing houses, using strips of veneer and wood. Whereas the girls preferred to use cardboard the boys attempted to make their own shells. This is where Stephen became interested. He desperately wanted to construct a house and on being encouraged to do so he settled down, to the relief of many of the other children. Perhaps the activity was so relevant to his own concerns that he needed to visualise it – he could not work on it in an abstract way.

Many creative activities were introduced to enliven the project. A most popular activity was the making of plaster of Paris models using sand as a mould. The children carefully painted the resultant plaques. A quantity of pieces of wire and ceramic resistors were placed in the classroom and a group of the boys made a collage which they called The Dangerous Machine, having talked about machines and their use on the site.

Because of the integrated nature of the project, many aspects of the curriculum were brought in. We looked at houses in Palestine and the reasons for their design, and made three-dimensional models of houses out of Lego. A story called 'The Iron Man' by Ted Hughes was read in instalments and the children made collage pictures of their impression of an Iron Man. This led to the investigation of the properties of nails and the question of rusting. The class talked of home and the homeless and looked at literature received from Dr Barnardo's homes. In physical education and movement and dance the class tried to think of weight-bearing parts of the body and danced to the sound effect of machines at work. They were also led to look at symmetry and the effect of design and overall appearance.

The worth of the project could only be assessed by firstly looking at the work done by the children and at the effect upon the classroom environment, and secondly by talking to the children and noting the effect of the whole on individuals and on the classroom climate. It seemed that a great deal of interest and indeed fun had been derived from the project as a whole; the points at which basic skills had been practised were numerous and the children were more knowledgeable than at the beginning of the project (which had covered a period of four weeks). The advantages of using the environment in a positive and tangible way became clear as the children began to relate personal experiences to the work done in the classroom. This raised an interest and, consequently, enthusiasm in the children; even Stephen found that being in school could be enjoyable – with his contribution to the classroom environment being valued rather than deprecated. The class, as a social group, found that there were difficulties in working closely with others, but having resolved these difficulties it is to be hoped that they will go on to co-operate in other situations. From the teaching point of view the project was flexible and interesting, providing many opportunities for teaching new things.

9 Creative and aesthetic experiences

What an explosion there has been in our schools in opportunities for children to experience space, materials and music. Opportunities to dance, explore and manipulate media have become an integral and readily accessible part of most daily programmes. Many classrooms and practical areas have become a kind of Aladdin's cave with sand, water, clay, wood, boxes, cardboard, paper and a huge variety of other plastic, malleable and pliable objects to construct, manipulate and make marks with. These materials are usually organised with care and precision in designated areas or labelled containers. Conversely some classrooms resemble supermarkets that have met with some major disaster or at least have got their stocks hopelessly muddled!

There is great pressure upon teachers to present children with opportunities to use their imagination. Teachers search avidly for 'new' ideas for using materials. Perhaps they need not be quite so anxious, for many children delight in re-exploring the properties and potentials of paint, dough, clay and crayon. It is only perhaps to keep an interest alive or extended that additional approaches need be suggested.

Art and craft

One hesitates to label so narrowly the activities which develop from these foundations. Indeed creative experience is fundamental to the young child, for before he can articulate them sufficiently well or can write he will express many of his ideas and thoughts through art and craft. Instead of the stereotypes many of us were expected to copy during our school days he will mostly enjoy uninhibited freedom to develop his own work, while at the same time being extended and stimulated by the teacher's questions. We are appreciating more and more the great contribution this aspect of the curriculum can make to imaginative and cognitive development. The following list indicates some of the reasons why 'creative' experiences are considered important:

(a) At the simplest level it encourages gross and fine motor development
(b) It explores concrete and imaginative experiences
(c) It helps emotional stability
(d) It is an aesthetic and kinaesthetic experience
(e) It gives points of growth for development in its broadest sense

Picture John – new to school. He is aggressive, noisy and frequently annoys other children by knocking their buildings down. How different he became when he painted; a quiet calm intensely interested little boy whose whole demeanour changed. His work, far from being haphazard one-colour splashes, reflected great care. It was certainly painting that unlocked this boy's capacity to enjoy and benefit from his school experiences.

However, many of us have been conditioned to think of art purely as therapy – as an 'extra'. It can be much more. The quiet communication between oneself and a 'creative' experience is often a special reinforcement of self-awareness. It can be the half-way house between verbalising and writing about oneself and can be another major means of coming to terms with experience and making sense of the world. Much early work will just be completed for sheer fun but given the opportunity most children will symbolise the important people and events in their lives. For example Julia painted a man – just a round head and legs – who was her clever grandpa making her a doll's house for Christmas.

Using the children's work

Sometimes children do not produce tangible 'results', particularly if introduced to a new material. The group of six-year-olds who had never experienced clay before made all manner of marks, shapes and dents in it but pummelled it to disintegration. Similarly Georgina got so fascinated with her greatly improved control of scissors that she snipped away at velvet and cotton without any thoughts of making a collage like the other children around her. As the majority of nursery and first schools display large amounts of children's work nursery teachers especially can feel rather anxious about having 'results' to display. What can happen in this situation is that outlines of pictures are presented for children to fill in with paint or little bits of paper. This would be regrettable if it hastened the stage when a child says 'I cannot draw such and such', thereby eroding the basic worth of these experiences, the process itself. Most young children if given the opportunity and time will produce recognisable symbols of people and things. In fact one defies any group of adults to produce more elephantine elephants than those crayoned by a group of six-year-olds after a story about this animal. What a pity if a template had been passed around such a group!

Alongside flexible opportunities for individual art and craft work the teacher will gradually introduce to the class suggested areas for development. She might request that within the next few days all the children made a print from a finger painting so that these could be used as covers for their mathematics book. She might require volunteers to re-paint the outside of a 'junk' box, or ask a group for ideas about what kind of wall decoration they would like to make for the home corner to follow last term's apple-printed wallpaper. The six- and seven-year-olds who had enjoyed interpreting the sparkle of bonfire night had this experience extended and reinforced by watching, at a safe distance, the colours and sparks of the blow lamp being used to repair the school gates. Everyone then hunted for glittering and shiny materials. Much beautiful work emerged: jewelled boxes, sequined felt patterns, gold and silver pictures and interesting tales which were told and written about castles and treasures.

It would be a mistake to think of creative experiences in a single dimension. For example constructional work might also involve estimation, balance, juxtaposing shapes, fine motor skills, patience as glue dries, and, if the child was working in a group, social, language and co-operative skills.

Usually by the time children are eight (if they have had plenty of previous experience) they will demand much more from their creative work. Increasingly they will want to work with greater precision. They want to know exactly how things work, the relationship between one event and another, what happened in the past and what could happen in the future. Their drawings reflect this. They enjoy making detailed plans and maps and diligently research to find out the exact details of, for example, a Roman legionnaire's uniform. They like collecting things and start to develop special interests. In other words their work reflects their increasing knowledge of time, space, materials and people. It must be emphasised that it would be a mistake not to let them express themselves freely through materials. They will still need this kind of emotional and cognitive support. Despite the fact that Piaget's concept of stages reinforces the need for children to continue to have practical experiences, many classrooms at the eight-year-old stage and particularly above this become increasingly imaginatively barren. For example the opportunity of drawing before one writes, with the great support and essential framework this gives to many children, is swept away as being unnecessary and possibly a waste of time. Not all children will need this kind of support but some may well still do so as their bored, lethargic or still tenuous attempts at written symbolic work testify.

The display and presentation both of the children's work and also of natural and man-made materials on interest, discovery and nature tables is, as already stated, of paramount importance. Many teachers have become really skilful display artists. Despite this there is a danger that full use will not be made of the work. It helps if children can put up some of their own work – one imaginative teacher has a wall space for this. Naturally it will be sufficient for some displays to be enjoyed purely as aesthetic experiences but the majority will be 'working' displays, evolving, developing and being constantly referred to. It is always a good idea if teachers can put up the work while children are watching so they are more directly involved. The rather stilted early reading book type of written label accompanying this work – for example 'here is a little boy', 'this is John's cat' – has largely been replaced by a more natural and interesting use of language – 'John's cat is washing its whiskers'. Frequently because nursery teachers have constantly resisted the pressure from above to teach skills of reading and writing children in nurseries live in a strange wordless world. Perhaps the teachers fear that introducing a few words will bring a tidal wave of stilted introductory reading books in its wake. It seems most odd, even if understandable, that displays are not labelled. Even something as individual as one's name gets translated into a picture, a daisy or perhaps a train indicating a child's place for his coat. Why not the picture *and* the child's name, one wonders? Surely the sooner children see the relevant use of written symbols the better. It need not be in the least cramping and would be an early introduction to the development of future skills.

Music and movement

Anyone who has long experience of working with children is likely to have noticed the very special response many children have when they sing. The lack of confidence that some children have when they speak disappears when they sing. The structure and melody form a reliable base on which they can express themselves. There are many opportunities for developing incidental music in the first school. Many young teachers can play the guitar and this is an ideal instrument for school use. The children will sing all sorts of songs for sheer fun: rhymes, traditional, nonsense songs and those relevant to current events. Children particularly enjoy personalised stories and songs. Many gifted teachers take the opportunity to reinforce, establish or develop a child's positive self concept by singing about him. Such essential matters as tidying the classroom are helped along by this type of singing. It is clear that the benefits of singing go beyond providing emotional, enjoyable social experiences. Our increasing understanding of the links between reading and writing helps us to understand how rhythm, pitch and the fine discrimination of sounds support articulation generally.

Probably the greatest influence on the development of music in schools, in its widest sense, has been Carl Orff. His use of the pentatonic scale and the beautiful musical instruments he has devised have led many children to experience very satisfying music. The way he has encouraged children to project their voices by singing their own names or words has done much to reinforce confidence, rhythm and melody. Music tables are frequently to be found in corners of classrooms or in corridors. Nursery and first school children are encouraged to make their own contributions to these 'sound' tables, by making rattles and shakers. These handmade instruments are of value but it would be a pity if Orff's instruments were not available too, as these guarantee success. There is now equal opportunity for both boys and girls to explore these and other percussion instruments (for in the past triangles and tambourines were considered appropriate for girls; drums, cymbals and castanets were a boy's province). The traditional concept of the 'percussion band' has largely been abandoned as too restrictive. Because we seem to be surrounded by indiscriminate noise often of a musical nature it is important that the children have the opportunity to listen to more carefully selected music. Sometimes the period before the beginning and at the end of assembly is used for listening to gramophone records. In one urban school a group of three hundred children would often quietly hum their favourite tunes – a sight and sound to be cherished.

Movement usually plays an important role in the first school. It is yet another valuable means of expression, a communication of one's inner self and a means of exercising increased bodily control. Initially movement lessons are concerned with space, control, speed and rhythms and usually the teacher uses her voice or a tambour to indicate changes in pace and direction. Gradually, after considerable experience, music is linked to the movement. Perhaps only snippets will be used – like the passage of the court entrance from Prokofiev's 'Lieutenant Kije'; one class would all pretend to be highly important people swishing their 'cloaks' as they paraded around the hall. This really appealed to Mark who was always requesting the 'important' music. He sometimes suggested we behaved importantly if we ever had to queue for any reason; others must have wondered why thirty-six people were all standing with their noses in the air looking aloof and nonchalant! This does illustrate how this boy was linking event to event. Another favourite passage was from Herb Alpert's version of 'The Girl from Ipanema', the lovely smooth flowing passage followed by bright jangly sounds.

Movement can become more and more closely linked with drama. The Gerald Rose story of 'The Big River' provides obvious dramatic movement opportunities. In this story the rain splashing on the mountain tops gradually develops into a trickle, stream, brook and then a river which flows into the sea. The children can make the appropriate moans and howls as the waves lash the seashore and be the fast-moving rivulet weaving its course down the mountain side.

Drama

Children will switch naturally from reality to make believe play, representing their experiences in appropriate action or words. This symbolisation of fact and fantasy hardly needs formal provision, since many aspects of the first school curriculum provide opportunities for it. It can become a deeper experience if certain materials and opportunities are available:

1 Dressing-up clothes including hats and uniforms
2 Puppets and theatre with materials for making one's own puppets
3 Occasions when the experience of watching 'good' children's theatre companies can be shared in schools
4 Whole group opportunities to dramatise action songs, rhymes and stories
5 Chances to act out fears and aggressions, as illustrated by changing the home corner into a surgery

Children need these fortifying, reassuring and expressive opportunities for 'make-believe play, day-dreaming, chatting about experiences, gossip, travellers' tales and storytelling . . . drama and poetry' (Britton 1970).

By judicious choice of stories and music for movement, more deliberate opportunities for drama can be incorporated into the school curriculum. The way drama is introduced will depend on the general level of development and experience of the children. Three- to five-year-olds will be largely egocentric in their behaviour and are likely all to want to be father bear, or endeavour to huff and puff and blow the pig's house down, so the stories should present such opportunities. Gradually, because the teacher wishes the children to experience co-operation, times will be initiated when the class will watch some of the group acting a favourite or impromptu story. One wonders what Arthur Lowe would have thought of Eddie and Stephen's version of 'Dad's Army'. Eddie drew a plan of campaign on a small board and instructed the home guard – the rest of us – in our duties. It was very amusing and ended with a lot of laughter. Seven- and eight-year-olds, seeking a more accurate representation of the world, may well be ready to write, direct and act their own dramas. Children will certainly enjoy the experience of using the range of their voices: they can be taught to stage whisper, thereby fostering careful diction and fine auditory discrimination.

Expressing one's feelings through glove and shadow puppets is less intensely direct than more public drama performed in front of a group. Some children feel considerably protected by the screen and therefore more readily explore their ideas and feelings.

There will be considerable interflow from and to various aspects of the curriculum. For example, drama becomes linked with movement when children use their whole bodies to respond to a feeling, evoke past experiences or dramatise a sequence of music or story.

Story

Although story telling has been mentioned in the development of language skills it is also considered appropriate to discuss it within this context. Schools should present numerous opportunities for listening to stories and poetry. These can comfort, provoke, exhilarate, provide fearful moments and illustrate human behaviour without moralising. They provide us with substantial touchstones for our own identity. The beauty of the language, the amazement at what others do, the magic of faraway events and places frequently incorporate elements of aesthetic experience. The warmth of the close contact between the teacher and her class makes each child feel as though the words are for him. The teacher who uses a range of tone, intonation, expression, tempo and gesture provides a framework for the quality of the child's own eventual silent reading.

Original works of art

Some local educational authorities run loan schemes for schools to borrow works of art. Others encourage schools to purchase their own original paintings, sculptures or pots. All these things increase a child's chances to see artists' work. These works, along with the carefully considered textures, colour schemes, furnishings and opportunities to see displays of craftsmanship ought to help foster discrimination.

One authority held an annual picture sale. A teacher who attended such an exhibition to help select paintings for her school told her class about her experiences. The children suggested that they had an exhibition of their own. This evolved into a rewarding activity with a portrait exhibition as the central theme. The class painted self-portraits or pictures of each other. The children were requested to bring photographs from home for the catalogue which was to contain the artists' biographies. The teacher discovered a real interest and desire in parents to co-operate – everyone found a photograph of some kind. (The teacher had planned to take additional photographs of individuals who could not supply them but this proved to be unnecessary.) The exhibition was mounted in the main entrance hall. Small groups of children took charge of it for short periods during the mornings and showed visitors around. So painting, reading, writing, social interaction and chances for increasing self-esteem were some of the benefits which arose from an initial shared experience.

Also there has been outstanding development in the presentation, quality of illustration and content of children's books. The variety is enormous and gives children and teachers great joy.

10 Facilities and resources

Although the explosion of the use of hardware in the nursery and first schools is not so large as that in secondary schools teachers of younger children have not failed to see the interesting possibilities in some of this equipment. Television, tape recorders, typewriters and instamatic cameras are now valued pieces of equipment in many schools.

Television and radio

Frequently teachers use television with three- to five-year-olds to maintain a strong link with home. It must be a comfort to some children, who are just starting school, that despite the unfamiliarity of many aspects of school life they can still watch favourite programmes designed for them. What is more they can share this experience with a larger group of children and the teacher who perhaps has more time and opportunity to discuss the programme than some parents. Some schools rarely have mass group viewing but place the television in a quiet corner so that small more intimate groups may watch it, perhaps with a parent, teacher's aide or nursery nurse.

There are many excellent school programmes for the five- to eight-year-olds. These are deliberately conceived to supply interesting information and give suggestions for things to do before and after the broadcasts. If fully exploited these programmes widen the children's horizons and add another dimension to the curriculum.

Stories, songs and poetry are broadcast on the radio for this age range. Listening in this way can be a new experience for those children who have previously only watched television or heard popular music broadcasts. Here the teacher becomes a member of the audience sharing the pleasures of a well-told tale. The children and teacher can observe each other's reactions closely, exchanging knowing smiles and nods, and thus experience a new intimacy.

Typewriters and tape recorders

Some schools are fortunate enough to have typewriters with a specially designed large typeface, while others make use of second-hand ones. Using the typewriter to practise phonics or write stories is a great motivator. Collectively children seem to enjoy this kind of machinery. It frees them, as does the *Breakthrough to Literacy* scheme, from using the mechanical skill of handwriting. They will have to search for letters, sometimes with the aid of a friend. It is not so laborious as it sounds and often tempts a child to be more adventurous in his writing.

Tape recorders are enormously useful in schools and many teachers are ingenious in devising ways of using them. The teacher will often record on cassette tape a story she has told to the whole group. Children can then resavour the experience by playing the story back to themselves on a simple playback machine. If the story is from a book this will be available for the child to look at as he listens. So that the children can hear other voices the teacher may get some other adult to record some stories. As a more deliberate attempt to develop reading skills she may record simple reading books, again with supplies of books for children to follow. She will devise some method of telling the children to turn the page without distracting them too much from the text. Three or four children, by using headsets, can listen and 'read' together.

Perhaps one day a machine will be invented which would write the children's stories, in clear print, as they told them. At the moment children, before they have acquired writing skills, can often tell very long and complex stories which are difficult for the teacher to write down in full for them. What can happen, because we want their drawings and stories to link with reading skills, is that we only take down a snippet of the story in writing. In this way we may be unwittingly programming the children to think that 'school writing' need only consist of short sentences. To alleviate this problem the teacher will sometimes tape record a child's whole story. Parents enjoy listening to these efforts when they collect their children at tea time (if they are able to). They are often amazed at their child's ability and sometimes want to know if a teacher told a child what to say. Occasionally the school secretary or some parents are asked to transcribe these stories so that they can be collected into a child's book or folder. After the initial shock of hearing what they sound like most children enjoy these experiences, and often this is reflected in the quite rapid improvement in the quality of their responses and ideas.

A major use of the tape recorder is the opportunity it presents to the teacher to record classroom interactions and then listen in isolation from the intimacy of the situation to what is really happening. Unlike the human ear the tape recorder is not selective! We are able to make a more dispassionate appraisal. Most adults have a natural instinct for inserting, correcting and extending children's language. Because of this we may not have observed the level of a child's speech with sufficient clarity. Recording a child talking at various times and in different contexts would be a valuable addition to other forms of recording progress. It could tell us much about that child's development. Although a tape recording cannot convey a complete picture of the teacher's behaviour it will show her intonation, speed of expression and subtle variations in her manner of addressing various children. Thus it tells her a lot about her *own* patterns of behaviour, which often operate below the level of consciousness. Perhaps this often sobering exercise will help to point her more positively in the direction of enabling children fully to express themselves. In the past talking skills, because they provided less tangible evidence for public display, have been undervalued in schools. Now, more than ever before we realise the importance of talk. Perhaps these chances to display evidence of spoken language development will give added support for teachers to carry out their convictions.

Videotape recording machines and instamatic cameras

We are not aware of any first school fortunate enough to have a videotape recorder. Many teachers feel that this medium would be ideal for recording progress and demonstrating the quality of the experiences presented to children. It has most of the advantages listed in the section about tape recorders but with the added dimension of vision. It can also be used to separate speech from movement or vice versa – a particularly valuable exercise. This concentration upon one dimension of human behaviour makes close analysis possible. We can listen with 'thinking ears' or watch with 'thinking eyes'. It could be used to help children recall their own experiences. Instant records of classroom events or outings can also be made, using polaroid cameras. The immediacy of the results particularly suits young children's need for the constant feedback of experiences.

The language master

This machine is a modified tape recorder. A card with twin-track magnetic tape attached to it can be passed through the machine. This card has space for eight seconds of speech, but that can be cut down to any length. The teacher can write the words on the card which she speaks on one track of the tape. The child passes the card through the machine, which then 'speaks' the words while the child reads the words and picture at the top of the card. If desired, the child can then repeat the word out loud and record it on to the second track of the tape, so that when he puts the card back through the machine, he hears his own word or words. Thus the machine allows children to link visual and sound images and to check their own performance. One advantage of this machine is that the teacher is free to devise whatever type of language programme she feels best suits groups or individuals in her class. A major feature of the machine is that it will go on repeating information indefinitely. Permanent tapes can be designed for certain aspects of reading and listening practice. Richard, a four-year-old attending a nursery class, was observed working with such a machine. The tapes told a very short story about the class guinea pig. They asked for responses to various questions. Richard was fascinated by the sound, written words and process and repeatedly put the cards through the machine.

This type of equipment has many exciting possibilities and can provide useful additional help for teachers and children. It ought to be stressed that most teachers would see it as one facet of a rich and varied approach to language.

Overhead projectors, slides and cine films

Overhead projectors can provide extra stimulus for children's talking, writing and drawings. They can be used in a variety of ways: glycerine or vegetable oils mixed with coloured inks can be placed on glass sheets so that light shines through and produces fascinating moving images; patterns can be produced using fabrics, feathers and such things as skeleton leaves; children can write and draw on the transparent sheets and find it exciting to see the large projected images of their work; a teacher can develop a story with her class by placing cut-outs or drawings on the projector, and so on.

Taking photographic slides of the children's work means that occasionally these can be re-explored by the class. These visual aids will help children recall experiences and will stimulate talk. The teacher can take slides of the locality and of places to be visited. Her records of the children at work in slide and cine form will be of special interest to parents.

Teachers' centres

The majority of these centres have sprung up in the last ten years. Each one has its own way of catering for teachers' needs. Some are almost entirely work places, whereas others have much more of the flavour of a social centre incorporating several educational services. Whatever emphasis they take many teachers welcome the opportunity to obtain information and cross reference their ideas with teachers of similar-aged children and those teaching other age ranges.

Many centres provide a location for pooling expensive resources, some of which can be hired out to schools for varying periods. Few first and small schools have the aid of a technician, so the centre's technician will be required to share his expertise. The centres have become places where information can be collected, debated and sometimes processed for distribution to teachers. Many centres have working parties enquiring into special aspects of teaching or the curriculum. These have become useful sounding boards for new approaches and feeders to reseachers and other teachers about interesting classroom practices.

PART III

11 Ways in which a teacher of young children copes with problems

Krishnamurti (1955) wrote:

The right kind of education is not possible *en masse*. To study each child requires patience, alertness and intelligence. To observe the child's tendencies, his aptitudes, his temperament, to understand his difficulties, to take into account his heredity and parental influence and not merely regard him as belonging to a certain category – all this calls for a swift and pliable mind, untrammelled by any system and prejudice. It calls for skill, intense interest and above all, a sense of affection.

Most teachers concerned with education in the early years would support these compelling words. The dedicated work that many teachers carry out in school is echoed by this quotation. However, in order to cope with problems, to know each child and assess the worth of the opportunities we present to him, monitor not only his progress but everyone else's, plan projects, select appropriate books, make apparatus, develop co-operative activities with colleagues and evaluate our overall effectiveness takes a great amount of time and effort. These ever-increasing demands upon teachers create difficulties. Dedicated teachers will try somehow to find the time but could do with more support – and all teachers vary in the amount of stress – and work – they can cope with. There have been numerous suggestions that in order to make teachers' responses to these demands more equal some form of contract should be devised making time before and after school, and preparation days prior to the commencement of school after holidays, a compulsory part of the job. (Many teachers do such things quite voluntarily, but less committed teachers may make minimal efforts.)

A teacher would try to respond to and cope with her children without prejudice. The day to day contact usually over at least a year (or in the case of vertical grouping two or three years) is a major force for fostering children's growth. Not only has the timetable become more flexible but also children have an opportunity for a close relationship with one adult. Many of the problems associated with teaching in secondary schools scarcely affect the first school. Children are not moved around from teacher to teacher for thirty- or forty-minute periods once a week. The great advantage for the nursery or infant teacher is that she can see a child's gradual developmental progress and be personally involved in this from day to day. The inappropriate labelling of a hierarchy of subjects indicating some as more worthy than others so prevalent in many secondary schools does not apply either. The teachers share equal status for they are not 'subject' teachers but teachers of children.

However, there are children with problems in nursery and infant schools, and strategies for coping with individual differences have been part of the subject of this book. We feel that it would be valuable at this point to make explicit some of the problems associated with early childhood education. It should be stressed that we, like most sensitive teachers, deplore the negative destructive labelling of children. At its worst whole families can be labelled as 'feckless', children condemned by such deplorable terms as 'thick' before they ever reach school, with the result that the teacher has a low level of expectation for the children. Expectations can become self-fulfilling prophecies. Hopefully this type of negative labelling is dying out, but it would be intolerable if it were replaced with other forms of pigeon-holing people. We adults are reinforced and encouraged by those who listen to us with intelligent interest but often utterly cast down by those who hold a poor opinion of us. Positive expectation feeds and encourages our responses. It is the same with children – for they constantly refer to adults for support and approval, and therefore a teacher must decide in advance what she will consider acceptable behaviour.

When we are looking at children with problems in the three to eight age range, we have to accept that these problems are in effect pleas for help. It is true that any teacher, experienced or otherwise, faced with a new class will find some children who will test out her reactions to various types of behaviour – to find the boundaries each person imposes. Even some quite young children will seem particularly unkind on these occasions, readily detecting any hesitancy and inconsistencies. It is always best for the new teacher to be patient and positive, perhaps restricting some activities until she is more *au fait* with the equipment and children. A teacher getting angry will probably frighten some children and greatly please those who are testing her out. Some children feel tremendously powerful if they can force a teacher into angry emotional responses, though at the same time they can become quite frightened by these very responses.

Similarly it is always best to stop the class or gather them around you only when you have something interesting to say. No group of children is readily going to leave or stop an activity for a regular 'nagging' session. It is very much a repetition of the 'cry wolf' story. This can lead to a wearing vicious circle, where the teacher's threats have to become more and more elaborate – with resulting exhaustion and frustration for everyone. So most experienced teachers would try to use positive reinforcement, where they stop the class to hear something interesting or gather them together to view someone's 'good' work, thus encouraging not only quick responses but general effort. They would avoid whole group lectures on behaviour. For example, it is best for a teacher not to shout from one end of the room to instruct a child not to make a noise! Rather go and whisper this instruction in his ear.

A major feature in the first school is that the 'sense of affection' can be demonstrated explicitly. Physical contact, so frequently condemned as taboo in the past, is quite acceptable when children are young. Many forms of aggressive and disruptive behaviour are pleas for affection: a child is expressing in his behaviour what he cannot in words – 'take notice of me, love me'. Usually the worse the behaviour the greater the child's inner distress and longing. The nursery or infant teacher can take hold of that child's hand, sit him on her knee, hold him reassuringly when his own aggressive behaviour frightens him. She can work the system to accommodate all kinds of children, while remembering of course that she is responsible for all the children in her care. Thus she might hold a distressed or timid child's hand while she went around from group to group talking with the other children. During story time she may sit the disruptive child upon her knee, which is likely to have a calming effect upon him. She may give a persistent 'wriggler' a book to hold and have grouped nearest to her those children who might interfere with others.

A good teacher will be flexible enough in her attitudes to permit a timid or uncertain child to watch movement lessons until he is familiar with the routines. Teachers today ought not to make children do things in an unnecessarily forceful manner. Sometimes with a barely adequate explanation children are invited to remove most of their clothes to go for 'movement'. Is there any wonder that some might be terrified at the prospect? Many tears and tantrums can be prevented if children are reassured with details of what is going to happen. The child who finds the school day rather long also can be given information about what will happen before tea-time and time to go home.

There are days when problems seem to coincide. Here a sympathetic head teacher can alleviate some of the pressure by having a child or small group of children in her room. A parent helper, the nursery nurse or an ancillary helper's services are invaluable – but it must be stressed that most infant teachers still have to cope on their own. Often teachers will form their own liaisons and work together, perhaps sharing their classes for the occasional story or reinforcing a child's behaviour or work by sending him to show some other teacher his efforts. This is useful because the teacher is making the child feel more important when he is 'good' – rather than falling into the trap of making him feel important when he is 'naughty'. It is not a good idea to send children to another teacher with 'poor' work; humiliating a child is never conducive to his making a greater effort next time. Sometimes it might be useful to set a child apart for a short time to let him ponder on his misdeeds or deprive him temporarily of social contact or of an activity. This does not mean making him stand in the corner or most dangerous of all sending him out of the room, but perhaps letting him sit for a while on a large chair to think, or letting him hold the guinea pig for a moment (if the child is not feeling too angry). This is really withdrawing him from a situation which he is finding too difficult; providing a temporary respite from problems.

Nevertheless it would be unrealistic to say that all behaviour or learning problems are soluble. Children differ in their responses. Some may have learned apathetic or destructive behaviour by the time they reach school. Some home backgrounds may even have taught (however unwittingly) mistrust of adults and defensiveness against other children. The teacher will have a difficult task in rebuilding trust and co-operation. Conversely, other children from orderly and courteous home backgrounds may find themselves in discourteous confused classroom surroundings. Although we try to understand a child in the terms of his individual predicament we cannot always know why he behaves in a particular way. We can observe overtly aggressive or exceedingly withdrawn behaviour but we cannot know the covert anxieties many children experience. The child who is perhaps the most neglected in school is often the quiet 'good' conforming child whom so many teachers are thankful to have in their class. Such children may have an enormous but unextended potential. The most vulnerable child may find himself over-protected by his teacher who smothers him in her attempt to compensate for his lack of love (or what she considers to be lack of love) at home.

Understanding possible underlying sources of a child's difficulty in adjusting is the first step to coping. For *if* a teacher can see why, it helps her to be more emotionally detached and objective. (She will always have to resist the feeling that she personally is the object of a child's attacks.) School cannot possibly alleviate a child's desperate home conditions but it can attempt to be a sanctuary for children in acute distress. What can happen, though, is that the child with the least love, who is perhaps the least able and has the poorest clothes and care has an equally unhappy and harassing time in school. Because such children are often slow in responding both to the teacher and to school happenings in general, his teacher may subconsciously neglect him – and children like him – and concentrate on those who respond well to her and are more obviously rewarding. A teacher, too, needs to feel and see that she is being successful and be reassured about her efforts. It ought to be a major part of the head teacher's role to extend this support.

School can also be a frustrating place for the gifted child who needs challenging situations to tackle. However, the now much greater opportunity for self-chosen activities means that he has the chance to concentrate for long periods on his own interests, often posing many of his own problems. He may become a disruptive force in a class if his alertness is considered to be 'cheekiness' and some teachers may set out deliberately to suppress such a child into submissive conformity. So she will have to ask herself if her provisions are suitable – and if she is aware of her own behaviour.

We have emphasised in the discussion of vertical grouping and elsewhere how children will adopt a teacher's lead. Some five-year-olds are beginning to understand that certain children are different and need extra help. They seem perceptive about the teacher's responses to children with special needs, and frequently join in with encouragement which is gratifying for everyone. They will in any case echo the teacher's responses, agreeing (usually) that someone has tried hard with a piece of creative work or has been very 'good'.

Children who come to school with no previous experience of routine or orderliness may well find school bewildering. We have more words which are peculiar to school than perhaps teachers appreciate – movement, corridor, head teacher, classroom, P. E., dinner lady, apparatus, etc. We need to explain. On a practical note a child may set off to school without breakfast, he may be tired from lack of nourishment or from late night television viewing. Many teachers see that school milk is available from the start of the day – another instance of varying routines to meet individual requirements.

Of course if children are behaving persistently badly the teacher must ask herself if her provisions are appropriate. A child who is bored is a potential source of disruption. A child is less likely to be bored if he has more opportunities to choose what he wants to do. A teacher with a child or children in her class who have limited concentration spans or are impatient tries to anticipate their needs and will make special provisions. She will, in particular, anticipate trouble and intervene before disruption starts. The ways of organising and the types of provision now take greater account of the *recipient*. We try not to ask the impossible, for example, expecting a child to sit still and complete meaningless tasks which are irrelevant to him, or demanding that he be quiet for long periods. No longer do we present children with boring tasks – too many, too often or too long!

Teachers usually decide upon a few simple rules to help the smoother running of the class – such as putting your own work away; returning equipment to its boxes; trying to finish what you have started (with the five to eight range only); clearing away immediately any accidental spillages; taking care of equipment and books and using an ordinary voice (i.e. not shouting) generally throughout school. For although a first school is likely to be full of lively spontaneity a certain tranquility also needs to be fostered.

It is ironic but saddening that a rude and aggressive teacher can be surprised when a child behaves similarly (the teacher as a model of behaviour is discussed further in chapter 5). Children will learn prejudice, rudeness and discourtesy from us if this is what we present to them. Is it possible to preserve the goodness and happiness that so many first schools embody? Tagore wrote these moving words:

Children with the freshness of their senses come directly to the intimacy of this world. This is the great gift they have. They must accept it naked and simple and must never again lose their power of immediate communication with it. For our perfection, we have to be vitally savage and mentally civilised, we should have the gift to be natural with nature and human with human society. My banished soul sitting in the civilized isolation of town-life cried within me for the enlargement of the horizon of its comprehension, I was like the torn-away line of verse, always in a state of suspense, while the other line, with which it rhymed and which could give it fullness, was smudged by the mist away in some undecipherable distance. The inexpensive power to be happy, which, along with other children, I brought to this world, was being constantly worn away by friction with the brick-and-mortar arrangement of life, by monotonously mechanical habits and the customary code of respectability.

Of course a teacher must observe the minutiae of behaviour and personality but she has always to try to see children as 'whole' people and thus put her observations into a proper perspective. Surely the emphasis should be upon 'being human with human society' for this exemplifies the very essence of the good relationships embodied in many nursery and first schools. If the ethos is positive and supportive for children and teachers many of the major difficulties can be surmounted.

12 Further developments

Preventive 'medicine'

Within the nursery and first school the concept of remedial education is inapplicable, for one cannot remedy what has not happened. The principle of early identification of children who have various problems indicating future difficulties in coping either with life in general or with a skill such as reading in particular seems more appropriate. Many teachers with long experience of dozens of children are adept at identifying those who would benefit by extra attention. Those children hesitant in speech, slow in response, lacking in general and specific co-ordination, or withdrawn, those who have suffered long or frequent absences, many changes of school or of teachers may be those who need special support. Some L.E.A.s are considering providing additional weekend and evening courses for gifted children as this group can also experience problems and frustrations. Several areas with high immigrant populations have language centres where many supportive courses for adults, children, teachers and nursery nurses are held.

How can we possibly supply 'preventive' care for these children? While classes are large and nursery nurses short there will be no easy answer. At the national level the National Nursery Examination Board has begun one-year advanced courses for experienced N.N.E.B.s. It is planned that this extra training will concentrate upon children with special needs. Language development will take a prominent place in the course.

In the meantime how are schools coping? It is true that many first schools have teachers who are extra to the establishment, that is, they are not responsible for a class. The head teacher is free to use the services of these teachers as she wishes. They may help generally or pay particular attention to children with reading difficulties. There is no one set solution – rather must each school consider its own children's needs.

One idea which seems to have merit is to withdraw small groups for a morning, afternoon or hour-long session to a specially equipped room. In one adventurous school this was particularly inviting, a real Kia-ora (Maori for 'welcome'). This small intimate place resembled a comfortable sitting-room with floor cushions, decorative mirrors, domestic light fittings, curtains, carpets and really motivating equipment – things to spark off conversation and intrigue children (for example, prismatic kaleidoscopes, slinky moveable springs and paperweights with oil bases). Although it had this delightful equipment the overall impression of the room was one of tranquillity. Just five children met there with one teacher who listened with extra care, talked and chatted and provided interesting supportive experiences. Nevertheless it would be bad if such provision were to emphasise differences and produce barriers between children for it is important that they learn to accept all comers and integrate them into a truly comprehensive first school.

The support given to encourage travellers' (gypsies') children to attend school is another indication of our increased desire to provide for special groups. Enormous strides have taken place in our efforts to understand the problems of the multi-racial society. Groups of teachers and social workers have visited India and the West Indies to study the way of life there. In turn these teachers have shared these valuable insights with others responsible for immigrant groups.

Parents of the future

Several secondary schools support the idea of some form of education for their pupils in child development, community service or preparation for parenthood. Many adolescents however cannot view themselves as future parents because they are still too involved in present problems, but at least they can get to know more about young children. Over the past decade more and more secondary schools are sending their pupils out to visit nursery and first schools. The Bullock Report (para. 5.11–13) gives interesting examples of good practice. Additionally older pupils, particularly those who find writing onerous, can tape stories and present puppet plays for these children, thereby practising and reinforcing their own skills in meaningful contexts. Groups of young children can be taken in the other direction to visit secondary schools.

This type of policy using a combination of resources seems sensible. Older children can learn about younger children, and the converse is also desirable. In order to be successful, such projects require careful preparation, supervision and follow-up. Much closer liaison will be necessary if teachers of young children are not to feel imposed upon and the children overwhelmed by visitors. It is essential that these developments give regard to mutual benefits.

Pre-school developments

In a greater effort to make the provision fit the real needs of society and in particular of working mothers and one-parent families, several nursery schools are beginning to extend their hours and periods of opening. Units such as the Thomas Coram and Dorothy Gardner Centre provide diversified services for the whole family. Play groups, nursery, medical, recreational, practical services like launderettes, and social services are grouped together to serve young neighbourhood families. They aim to be especially supportive to parents. Few of these specially-built centres exist but many nursery head teachers and playgroup leaders are devising ways of helping mothers with their under three-year-old children. Some offer play facilities on one day a week, so that the mothers can meet socially or pursue activities for their own personal satisfaction. One of the most successful approaches forming closer links between parents, school and pre-school children has been the establishment of toy libraries. Here, once again, secondary pupils can be involved in making and repairing the toys, not merely at the production and care level but at that of making decisions about the suitability and safety of the designs. Going to school with mother to select a toy and story tape establishes links between home and school and helps to minimise the threat of the unfamiliar.

Alternative provision for pre-school children

For some children the step from home to school at three even with careful preparation is too great. At the moment we do not have alternative opportunities for these children. In France mothers are given some financial inducement to stay at home with their pre-school children. This could be very helpful for those mothers who wish to do this. In Sweden mothers who seem to have been successful with their own children are sometimes employed to take care of small groups of children in their homes. This provides a similar service to that given by a successful childminder. It means that these young children experience all the qualities of a 'good' home within a framework that has greater similarity to their experience. An alternative, for children of statutory school age, would be the development in schools of more small 'withdrawing' areas where children can feel less over-stimulated and more secure and able to develop concentration, but this would necessitate better staffing ratios.

Taking education into the community

Often in the twilight areas of our cities children lack play opportunities, but for a parent to trail a toddler and baby a longish distance to some centre might create even more problems than it solved. Several authorities run 'playbuses', which are converted buses equipped with play materials which take play opportunities to the children. The problem of the geographically isolated rural pre-schooler is not so easy to resolve but something of this nature seems a useful idea, the bus gathering groups of children together for sessions and then taking them home. For many, previous lack of companionship with children of their own age makes the transition to school difficult.

Conflicts and differences in opinion about appropriate approaches for different age groups will continue to be debated. They will not be easy to resolve, but perhaps some of the differences will be minimised when more emphasis is placed upon the developmental needs of individual children. In the best first schools, some of which have nursery classes attached, full advantage is taken of the extended period to develop a child's social and cognitive competence. Circular 2/73 (D.E.S. 1973) gave support to the concept of first schools by stating, partly on economic but principally on educational grounds, that it was desirable for children below the age of five to attend school in units attached to primary schools. This avoids a school change at an early age and ought to strengthen the dovetailing of early childhood education.

Much research evidence supports the desirability of offering the widest opportunities during a child's formative years for the development of skills and of a positive self-concept. There is also a growing and alarmingly naïve tendency to expect the provision and content of early childhood education, particularly in the pre-school sector, to be a cure-all for most social ills. On the merit side barriers of all kinds are being removed: hostility between playgroup leaders and professionally trained teachers is disappearing as they begin, or continue in some cases, to work closely and deliberately towards cohesive policies; both major political parties have pledged themselves to the eventual development of a full pre-school programme and most importantly many satisfactory developments, based on greater mutual respect and understanding are taking place in parent/teacher partnerships.

The rapidly changing pattern of society makes it more essential than ever that our schools prepare children to be adaptable in order to meet uncertain future demands. Thus there is a need for a flexibility of approach which will rely more upon ways of learning and tackling problems than upon transmission of factual knowledge. In addition the present needs of children have great relevance. It is important that account should be taken of their day-to-day satisfaction, for the means of achieving this will contribute to the establishment of future values and attitudes, and to their current well-being. The quality of living which is available for them during the early years is likely to have far-reaching effects.

References *and* Name index

BEARD, R. M. (1969) *An Outline of Piaget's Developmental Psychology.* London, Routledge and Kegan Paul. *26–7, 82, 113*

BEREITER, C. and ENGELMANN, S. (1966) *Teaching Disadvantaged Children in the Pre-School.* Englewood Cliffs, N. J., Prentice Hall. *69*

BLACKIE, JOHN (1967) *Inside the Primary School.* London, H.M.S.O.

BLACKSTONE, T. (1971) *A Fair Start,* London, Allen Lane.

BOARD OF EDUCATION (1933) *Report of the Consultative Committee on Infant and Nursery Schools* (Hadow Report). London, H.M.S.O. *7–8, 10*

BREARLEY, M. (1969) (ed.) *Fundamentals in the First School.* Oxford, Blackwell.

BRITTON, J. (1970) *Language and Learning.* London, Allen Lane, The Penguin Press. *60, 117*

BULLOCK REPORT See Department of Education and Science (1975).

CENTRAL ADVISORY COUNCIL FOR EDUCATION (ENGLAND) (1967) *Children and their Primary Schools,* vol. 1 (Plowden Report). London, H.M.S.O. *12–14, 15, 17, 18–19, 25, 42, 61*

CENTRAL ADVISORY COUNCIL FOR EDUCATION (WALES) (1967) *Primary Education in Wales* (Gittins Report). London, H.M.S.O. *15, 16*

CHAZAN, M. (1973) (ed.) *Compensatory Education.* London, Butterworths.

DEPARTMENT OF EDUCATION AND SCIENCE (1972) *Education: A Framework for Expansion.* White Paper. London, H.M.S.O. *14–15*

DEPARTMENT OF EDUCATION AND SCIENCE (1972) *Educational Priority,* vol. 1 *E.P.A. Problems and Policies,* ed. A. H. Halsey. London, H.M.S.O.

DEPARTMENT OF EDUCATION AND SCIENCE (1973) *Nursery Education Circular No 2/73. 138*

DEPARTMENT OF EDUCATION AND SCIENCE (1975) *A Language for Life* (Bullock Report). London, H.M.S.O. *61, 70, 73–5, 136*

DUNN, L. M. and SMITH, L. O. (1964) Peabody Language Development Kit. Nashville, Tennessee, Institute for Mental Retardation and Intellectual Development, George Peabody College for Teachers. *69*

ELVIN, L. (1969) The Positive Roles of Society and the Teacher. In R. S. Peters (ed.) *Perspectives on Plowden.* London, Routledge and Kegan Paul. *46–7*

FLETCHER, H. (1970) (ed.) *Mathematics for Schools, Level 1: Teacher's Resource Book*. London, Addison-Wesley. *93*

GABRIEL, J. (1968) *Children Growing Up* (3rd ed.). London, University of London Press.

GARDNER, D. E. M. and CASS, J. E. (1965) *The Role of the Teacher in the Infant and Nursery School*. London, Pergamon. *18, 48*

GATTEGNO, C. (1969) *Reading with Words in Colour*. Reading, Education Explorers. *75*

GITTINS REPORT See Central Advisory Council for Education (Wales) (1967).

HADOW REPORT See Board of Education (1933).

HUGHES, TED (1968) *The Iron Man*. London, Faber. *109*

JONES, J. K. (1967) *Colour Story Reading*, Teacher's Manual. London, Nelson. *75*

KELLMER PRINGLE, M. L. (1975) *The Needs of Children*. London, Hutchinson.

KRISHNAMURTI (1955) *Education and the Significance of Man*. London, Gollancz. *126*

MACKAY, D., THOMPSON, B. and SCHAUB, P. (1970) *Breakthrough to Literacy*, Teacher's Manual. Schools Council Programme in Linguistics and English Teaching. London, Longman for the Schools Council. *76, 121*

MILLAR, SUSANNA (1968) *The Psychology of Play*. Harmondsworth, Penguin. *81–2*

NATIONAL CHILD DEVELOPMENT STUDY (1972) *From Birth to Seven*. A report by R. Davie and others. London, Longman.

OWEN, R. (1920) *The Life of Robert Owen: written by himself*. London, Bell (reprint: 1st ed. 1857–8, London, Wilson). *2–3*

PITMAN, SIR J. and ST JOHN, J. (1969) *Alphabets and Reading: the initial teaching alphabet*. London, Pitman. *75*

PLOWDEN REPORT See Central Advisory Council for Education (England) (1967).

PLUCKROSE, H. (1975) *Open School, Open Society*. London, Evans. *87*

POTTER, BEATRIX (1907) *The Tale of the Flopsy Bunnies*. London, Warne. *67*

POULTON, G. A. and JAMES, T. (1975) *Pre-School Learning in the Community: Strategies for Change*. London, Routledge and Kegan Paul.

ROSE, GERALD (1963) *The Big River*. London, Faber. *116*

ROSEN, C. and ROSEN, H. (1973) *The Language of Primary School Children*. Schools Council Project on Language Development in the Primary School. Harmondsworth, Penguin Education for the Schools Council. *65*

SAUNDERS, M. (1976) *Developments in English Teaching*. London, Open Books. *61*

SCHAFFER, H. R. (1971) *The Growth of Sociability*. Harmondsworth, Penguin. *25*

SCHOOLS COUNCIL (1971) *Just Before School*, by M. Chazan, A. Laing and S. Jackson. First Report of the Compensatory Education Research and Development Project. Oxford, Blackwell. *69*

SCHOOLS COUNCIL (1972) *A Study of Nursery Education*, by P. H. Taylor, G. Exon and B. Holley. Working Paper 41. London, Evans/Methuen.

SCHOOLS COUNCIL RESEARCH STUDIES (1974) *Pre-school Education*, by M. Parry and H. Archer. Report of the Schools Council Project on Pre-school Education. London, Macmillan.

SEALEY, L. G. W. and GIBBON, V. (1965) *Beginning Mathematics*. Oxford, Blackwell. *93*

SHERIDAN, M. D. (1973) *Children's Developmental Progress* (new ed.). Windsor, N.F.E.R. *24*

SHORT, E. (1972) *Birth to Five*. London, Pitman.

SOCIAL SCIENCE RESEARCH COUNCIL (1975) *Early Childhood Education*, by B. Tizard (new ed.). Windsor, N.F.E.R. *16, 25*

TAGORE, R. (1931) *The Religion of Man*. London, Unwin Books. *132–3*

TIZARD, B. (1975) See Social Science Research Council (1975).

TOUGH, JOAN (1973) *Focus on Meaning*. London, George Allen and Unwin. *62*

VAN DER EYKEN, W. (1973) (ed.) *Education, the Child and Society*. Harmondsworth, Penguin.

VAN DER EYKEN, W. (1974) *The Pre-School Years* (3rd ed.). Harmondsworth, Penguin.

WARBURTON, F. W. and SOUTHGATE, (1969) *i.t.a.: An Independent Evaluation*. Report of a study carried out for the Schools Council. Edinburgh and London, Chambers and Murray. *75–6*

WEBB, L. (1974) *Purpose and Practice in Nursery Education*. Oxford, Blackwell.

WHITBREAD, N. (1972) *The Evolution of the Nursery-Infant School*. London, Routledge and Kegan Paul. *6*

WILKINSON, ANDREW (1971) *The Foundations of Language*. London, Oxford University Press.

Subject index